Chinese Animated Film and Ideology, 1940s–1970s

This book examines animated propaganda produced in mainland China from the 1940s to the 1970s. The analyses of four puppet films demonstrate how animation and Maoist doctrine became tightly but dynamically entangled.

The book firstly contextualizes the production conditions and ideological contents of *The Emperor's Dream* (1947), the first puppet film made at the Northeast Film Studio in Changchun. It then examines the artistic, intellectual, and ideological backbone of the puppet film *Wanderings of Sanmao* (1958). The book presents the means and methods applied in puppet animation filmmaking that complied with the ideological principles established by the radical supporters of Mao Zedong in the first half of the 1960s, discussing *Rooster Crows at Midnight* (1964). The final chapter discusses *The Little 8th Route Army* (1973), created by You Lei in the midst of the Cultural Revolution.

This book will be of great interest to those in the fields of animation studies, film studies, political science, Chinese area studies, and Chinese philology.

Olga Bobrowska is a scholar active in the fields of animation studies, film studies, and cultural theory, as well as a film culture activist and curator.

CRC Press Focus Animation Series

The Focus Animation Series aims to provide unique, accessible content that may not otherwise be published. We allow researchers, academics, and professionals the ability to quickly publish high impact, current literature in the field of animation for a global audience. This series is a fine complement to the existing, robust animation titles available through CRC Press/Focal Press.

Series Editor Chris Robinson is the Artistic Director of the Ottawa International Animation Festival (OIAF) and is a well-known figure in the animated film world. We welcome any submissions to help grow the wonderful content we are striving to provide to the animation community.

Giannalberto Bendazzi; Twice the First: Quirino Cristiani and the Animated Feature Film

Maria Roberta Novielli; Floating Worlds: A Short History of Japanese Animation

Cinzia Bottini; Redesigning Animation United Productions of America

Rolf Giesen; Puppetry, Puppet Animation and the Digital Age

Pamela Taylor Turner; Infinite Animation: The Life and Work of Adam Beckett

Marco Bellano; Václav Trojan: Music Composition in Czech Animated Films

Olga Bobrowska; Chinese Animated Film and Ideology, 1940s–1970s: Fighting Puppets

Chinese Animated Film and Ideology, 1940s–1970s

Fighting Puppets

Olga Bobrowska

CRC Press is an imprint of the
Taylor & Francis Group, an **informa** business

First Edition published 2023
by CRC Press
6000 Broken Sound Parkway NW, Suite 300, Boca Raton, FL 33487-2742

and by CRC Press
4 Park Square, Milton Park, Abingdon, Oxon, OX14 4RN

CRC Press is an imprint of Taylor & Francis Group, LLC

ISBN: 978-1-032-14889-2 (hbk)
ISBN: 978-1-032-14893-9 (pbk)
ISBN: 978-1-003-24160-7 (ebk)

DOI: 10.1201/9781003241607

Typeset in Minion
by Deanta Global Publishing Services, Chennai, India

In memoriam Professor Alicja Helman
(1935–2021)

Contents

Acknowledgments

I am wholeheartedly grateful to the numerous individuals and institutions who have supported but also constructively criticized my research, and as any other writer, I realize I will fail in naming them all in this place. My work started during the PhD studies at the Faculty of Management and Social Communication of the Jagiellonian University in Kraków (Poland), and only because of the encouragement, advices, and understanding received from my mentor, Professor Alicja Helman, did I persist in exploring the fascinating realm of Chinese cultural history. In her life and work, Professor Helman proved that all expected as well as unpredictable obstacles will always be overcome if one remains faithful to the principle of research integrity. I sincerely thank the academics who have first seen the potential of publishing this manuscript – the late Professor Giannalberto Bendazzi, Professor Marcin Giżycki (Polish-Japanese Academy of Information Technology in Warsaw, Rhode Island School of Design), and Professor Robert Sowa (Jan Matejko Academy of Fine Arts in Kraków). Communication, exchanges, and encounters with Dr. Chunning (Maggie) Guo (Associate Professor, Vice-Dean of Design Department, School of Art, Renmin University of China) and Professor Zhou Zhou (Southwest Minzu University in Chengdu) substantially shifted my initial recognition of the Chinese animation history and continuously inspired me. I am grateful to the CRC Press, especially Will Bateman and Simran Kaur, for their trust. I thank Waltraud

Grausgruber and Tricky Women/Tricky Realities Festival in Vienna for facilitating access to the essential research materials, Andrijana Ružić for empowerment. My family supported me unconditionally – Anita Bielańska, Kaja Kajder, Stefan Bielański, Bogumiła Bielańska, Ireneusz Bobrowski, and Ewa Bobrowska who I miss very much. I thank my husband Michał for everything.

Introduction

THIS BOOK PRESENTS FOUR analyses of the puppet films realized in mainland China in 1947–1973 that thematize communist revolution. The consecutive chapters discuss works that appear especially interesting for a complexity of historical, cultural, and ideological contexts they revoke: *The Emperor's Dream* (*Huangdi meng*, 1947) was made during the Civil War (1945–1949), and it presents a surrealist caricature of Chiang Kai-shek (Jiang Jieshi), the vilified leader of the Kuomintang (Chinese Nationalist Party, KMT) who governed in Taiwan until 1975; *Wanderings of Sanmao* (*Sanmao liulang ji*, 1958) is an adaptation of one of the most iconic *manhua* works authored by Zhang Leping; the anti-feudal fairytale, *The Rooster Crows at Midnight* (*Banye ji jiao*, 1964), is an adaptation of famous soldier Gao Yubao's autobiography; *The Little 8th Route Army* (*Xiao balu*, 1973) stands out as a coming-of-age, war and adventure, animated fiction resonating with the spirit of the Cultural Revolution. In all four cases, the narrative settings relate directly to the wartime era and 1949 Liberation effort. The aim here is to observe the process of infusing the animated film with particular meanings of the doctrine, or in other words, to understand how animated propaganda is constructed and executed. The analytical and interpretive activities depart from the questions regarding the changeability of the model of animated realism as a paradigm for visualizing and narrating the People's Republic

DOI: 10.1201/9781003241607-1

of China's (PRC) founding myth, i.e., the myth of Liberation as a revolutionary, collective, and grassroots effort.

VISIONS OF HISTORY IN CONTEMPORARY CHINESE ANIMATION

In the early 2010s, mainland China's art-house animation began circulating at the Western festivals. Conceptual, quite hermetic, and frequently of an intermedia character, the works of young animators from the PRC shattered generalized, exoticizing, and Western-centric assumptions about Chinese animation. Among numerous qualities manifested in this independent wave,[1] it is necessary to mention opening up towards new perspectives on animation's aesthetics and perception. These new films contested former conventions, technical mastery as a sole purpose of animation filmmaking, and sought possibilities of overcoming the emotional and intellectual communicative vacuum generated by the global, market-oriented processes that affected contemporary arts production in China. Importantly, these new voices have not come out of nowhere. Formally and politically bold, these films seemed to evoke and twist certain specific traditions that were already present for many years in the Chinese animated cinema. It was especially interesting to look at the Chinese culture's past through the images created by artists such as Lei Lei, Sun Xun, Chen Xi, and An Xu (1977–2017). After ten years, they have become the most acclaimed artists of the 2010s wave, whose films, multimedia installations, and other varied visual artworks hold a high position in the canon of contemporary arts.

The vision of history embedded in Chen Xi and An Xu's *Grain Coupon* (2011) appears the most self-explanatory. This 2D computer cut-out animation takes the viewer to the times of the Cultural Revolution and follows the dynamics of a violent relationship between a Red Guard, a forger, and his wife. Lines of the text on the screen inform about the historical setting. The visual and sound design rely on the conventions of caricature, shadow theater, and Chinese opera unveiling the variety of cultural traditions as an inspirational source of animation. The film can be read as a miniature treatise about the consequences of appropriation of a symbolic space by ideology-driven visuality. The main character of a forger is a virtuoso of his trade. Poverty and hunger force him to cooperate with the brutal fighter who keeps bringing him the following revolutionary artifacts for the purpose of forgery: Mao Zedong's portrait (denoting absolute values of the ideology), rare postage stamp (denoting values of revolutionary art), and the grain coupons (pragmatic symbol of an existential value). Contrarily to the overstylized and grotesque characters of the protagonists, the forged, propaganda images appear real, active, and powerful. On the critical level of reception, one notices that the visual world of ideological symbols neither represents nor relates to what can be observed in the reality experienced by the characters.

Sun Xun's artistic works vary in terms of employed media but they share a characteristic of being twofold narratives. On the one hand he presents wide, panoramic views on mythological dimension of historical time. On the other one, this artist from the northwestern, mining city of Fuxin, takes subjective, close look on the structures of the relationship between the power and the individual. While the animated woodcut graphics *Some Actions Which Haven't Been Defined Yet in the Revolution* (2011) remains arguably his most acknowledged film, it is also worth contemplating Sun's quasi-sociological project exhibited in 2014 in Singapore. *Republic of Jing Bang* was an 'experimental state' constituted for the period of six weeks where the 'citizens' (collectors) were acquiring their status along with the set of documents (passport, visa, identity card), tokens of the state's identification (maps, flag, anthem) as well as various paintings, posters, and other graphic works conveying core contents of Jing Bang's national mythology. According to the regulations and guidelines of the republic, the lie was a dominant discourse of Jing Bang, thus Sun Xun's limitless visual imagination not only encouraged to search for double coding but even directly demanded revisionist and critical attitudes from the participants. Among the souvenirs exposing 'Jing Bang's artistic traditions' one finds woodcut that presents Monkey King, the most iconic character of the classic Chinese animation. The poster with the Monkey's visage relates directly to the canonical depiction from *Havoc in Heaven* (*Danao tiangong*, 1961–1964, dir. Wan Laiming). The slogan accompanying the poster reads: "We are No Longer Political Toys". Parodying the rhetoric and communication codes of the PRC Sun Xun summoned the 'citizens': "What we should be doing is inventing history rather than establishing a country!" (Sun 2).

Lei Lei, the author of *Recycled* (2012), is another 'inventor' of the history. In cooperation with French photographer Thomas Sauvin, Lei Lei animated 3,000 photos selected from more than half a million, scanned, 35 mm color film negatives that were found at the garbage sites around Beijing. Abounded pictures present the individuals posing in front of historic and touristic sites, attending formal celebrations as well as family holidays and reunions. The photographs traverse through a threefold split screen in a rhythm dictated by sound reminiscing of the underground train's rumble. This specific audiovisual hypnosis evokes consideration for convoluting contradictions that establish interpretative framework of the film: an imperative of documenting the history (personal and societal) is confronted with the fact that the memory of the photographs is lost at the garbage site, the memory of the individuals is as ephemeral as photographic film, both decay alike eventually; the portrayed characters affirm individuality with their facial expressions, gestures, and postures, and yet they all mimic themselves and keep reproducing the same conventions of behavior, in the course of editing manipulations they lose individuality and become a uniform mass.

Chinese independent animation finds its artistic identity in experimentation understood as acts of creativity and reception, both stimulating intellectual opening up towards inspirations and interpretations valid in the fields of anthropology, reflection on politics, ideas, and history. The encountered, dispersed metaphors are comprehensible for the viewers from outside of the Chinese cultural context; nevertheless, the PRC remains their major point of reference as a myth and an icon, a trauma of the past, future dilemma, and today's confusion. Chinese experimental animators do not portray the PRC as a particular, socio-political structure but rather as a visual and narrative entity perplexed with the notions of nostalgia and resentment. While their creative predecessors conjoined the animated film language with an ideological discourse of the Maoist doctrine remolded accordingly to its changeable trajectory, the contemporary filmmakers seem to examine the extent of ideological criticism's applicability in a cinematic form of such inheritance.

INITIAL PREMISES

The presented research was instigated by the appreciation of the contemporary Chinese animation's multifaceted rhetoric that regards a vision of history and deconstructs symbols of the past collective imagination. However, the concern here is limited to the production realized in the Maoist era of the 1940s–1970s, i.e., the period of the cultural production's extreme subjugation to the doctrine formulated by Mao Zedong.

The majority of the classic era, SAFS' (Shanghai Animation Film Studio, *Shanghai meishu dianying zhipian chang*) production directly targeted children's audience with the films built upon fairytale, anthropomorphized representations. Maoist children's film is a substantially varied material; thus its reading may facilitate a discussion on narratives regarding ideological, intellectual, and aesthetic transformations occurring within the mainstream of the Maoist China's culture production. Animation was supposed to simplify and transmit the doctrine's contents of an educational, behavioral, and indoctrinating character. The most well-recognized and appreciated artistic strategies of the SAFS animators (trends of *minzu*, national, style) had to seek validation in terms of ideological usefulness even if the animators themselves were rather interested in technical uniqueness and innovative craftsmanship. The animations which directly conveyed propagandistic contents and whose imagery belonged to the reservoir of socialist symbolism and narratives (war, enemy, revolution, industrialization, etc.) are rarely discussed by scholars, curators, or festival programmers. The presented monograph fills this niche as it chooses to focus on an overtly ideologized animated film production.

Contextual and historicized analyses of the films made at the SAFS during the Maoist era, prove that the Chinese animated film has never presented itself as an ideological monolith. Watching classic Chinese animations requires substantial shifts in terms of reception habits. The viewers approaching Chinese animation heritage and anticipating traits of an 'artistic contraband'[2] typical for other contexts of socialist film production, quickly find themselves confused. Instead of procuring imageries and narratives potentially inclined to dissidence, the Shanghai animators sought themes, forms, and means of expression that would simultaneously universalize and conform to the accepted meanings of the dominant doctrine. Critical analysis of the films may unravel however the inner tensions and fluctuations within the ideological discourse regulating artistic communication in Mao's China.

The films discussed here depict the historical reality of the years 1931–1949. Plot development of these films revolves around the themes of mass resistance (military actions, grassroot struggles against the oppressors, guerilla revolution). Another variation is the films presenting historical characters related to the Communist Party of China (CPC) or Kuomintang. Such themes are directly connected with the prime agenda of the Chinese communist revolution, i.e., equation between national cause and global, communist revolution.[3] The material allows one to observe a tendency for universalization of the presented vision of history. Disinclined to represent individual characters and events, their penchant for anonymization of heroic deeds serves to objectify the historical process.[4] Focus on a particular technique – in this case, the puppet film (*mu'ou yingpian*) – helps to trace ideologically motivated changes in aesthetics and rhetoric. The basic rules of all propaganda communication require constructing the 'us-them' dichotomy; therefore, the analyses demonstrate normative, representational patterns employed in the construction of the positive and negative characters. The intention here is to establish a catalog of the 'eternal laws' regulating the conventional animated representations of pre-Liberation China and to indicate these ideas within the doctrine which were appraised by the propaganda apparatus as needed in the nation-building process.

The Maoist ideology determined production conditions and artistic agenda pursued at the SAFS. Due to the PRC's geopolitical position in the reality of the Cold War era, the Chinese artists were to a large extent isolated from the international circulation of trends, tendencies, and filmmaking innovations. The transcultural perspectives in studying the history of Maoist ideas and arts cannot be underestimated; nevertheless, the SAFS animators had to learn and master their skills mostly without confronting their works with the audiences unaccustomed to the Chinese traditions. Chinese animation emerged from the Wan brothers' persistence and personal engagement.[5] In the early 1920s, they went against the film industry (predominately based on foreign capital) and dictated their own terms in experimenting with frame-by-frame camera. On the one hand, the Wans were busy with the production of commissioned cartoons (*katong*) and special effects,[6] and on the other, they were thrilled to experiment (*shiyan*) in order to create anti-Japanese propaganda:

> The reason we were able to use the weapon of fine arts as an anti-imperialist tool and participate in patriotic movements, to allow animation to enter the ranks of anti-Japanese, was because we were influenced and educated by progressives from the literary and artistic world.
>
> (WAN AND WAN 57, QTD. IN MACDONALD 17)

Importantly, both areas of Wan brothers' explorations possessed well-defined target audience: it was a Chinese viewer who was interested in the cinema (still novel and mysterious, a highly attractive medium) and who expected it to deliver contents that would represent the Chinese reality either with the use of modern means of artistic expression that evolved in the period of the 'Chinese Enlightenment' or as related to the values and stories characteristic for the Chinese cultural traditions.

The process of sinicization of the cinema production appears as paradigmatic for the history of Chinese animation. It embraces phenomena such as overtaking means of production and distribution, development of the styles rooted in the aesthetic habits of the Chinese audiences, evolving of the narrative and representation models grounded in the cultural codes easily recognizable for the Chinese receivers. The movie camera, a 'Western colonizers' invention', granted means of a massified, propaganda communication, a feature quickly acknowledged by the Chinese political leaders (especially left-wing affiliated). Overtaking means of film production (along with animation) implied undertaking of two symbolic and discursive activities: elimination of the artistic practices that would echo the outside China's provenience of the medium and integration of the new strategies with the principles of the dominant (Maoist) doctrine.

Another significant characteristic of the filmmaking practice conducted at the SAFS in the Maoist period was the collectivization of the creative and production process. This strategy made the Chinese animators reluctant towards *auteur* practices. The vision of the world mirrored in the films made at the SAFS was a universal vision of the Maoist culture production apparatus and not a result of individual pursuits centered on artistic subjectivism and avant-garde approach. Animation functioned as a tiny screw in the greater machine of culture production; therefore, it is necessary to examine the machinery's provenience, structural components, and modes of functionality designed by its engineers. The presented reflection about the history of a specific film form (puppet animation) that thematizes the nation's heroic struggle against past oppression intertwines with the study of the history of Maoist ideas regarding culture and arts. This research presents the impact of the politics on the animated film art by reconstructing the processes that either reduced or enlarged the areas within which an ideologized medium launched utterly new realities.

MAOIST CHINA'S CULTURAL HISTORY: A BRIEF OVERVIEW

In order to discuss the vision of history manifested in particular culture texts, it is necessary to establish a framework for understanding the changes occurring on the cultural history timeline. Inevitable simplifications serve the purpose of drawing the panorama of threshold events at the background of wider, transformative processes.

The year 1949 addressed as Liberation, stands as a symbolically powerful, demarcation point on the 20th-century mainland China's timeline. On October 1, 1949, Mao Zedong proclaimed the founding of the People's Republic of China from the Heavenly Gate at the Tiananmen Square, thus sanctioned the political, ideological, and cultural existence of the entity of 'New China' (*Xin Zhongguo*). The period of Maoist dictatorship symbolically ended with the death of the Great Helmsman on September 9, 1976. The Third Plenary Session of the Eleventh Central Committee of the Chinese Communist Party held in December 1978 established the principles of the new social and political order, subjugated to the concepts of modernization, reforms, and opening up. Both Maoist and modernization heritage remains an integral element of the socio-political construction of the current 'great renaissance of the Chinese nation' (*Zhonghua minzu weida fuxing*). This book focuses on the concern of animation in Maoist times and it will not address the concerns of post-Maoist and 'post-socialist' culture, 'Cultural Fever', Chinese postmodernism, or more recent occurrences. Given the themes found in the source material, the presented discussion traces the intricacies back to the pre-1949 culture.

Mao Zedong has frequently defined pre-Liberation China's[7] political, economic, and social system as non-democratic, semi-colonial, semi-feudal, and suffering from imperialist oppression. On the one hand he recognized that between 1912 and 1949, the state depended on capitalist social organization of the urban areas controlled by the foreign powers (allowing for a limited participation of the Chinese nationals in the capital-generating endeavors), while on the other, the system relied on feudal structures of power and labor organizing the life in the provinces. The political geography of early 20th-century China did not breathe optimism – in addition to the limited agency over the resourceful but colonially dependent, port cities, the central, republican government was weakened by the external conditions as well as was guilty of corruption. Furthermore, the leaders of the ruling party, Kuomintang, neither commanded nor regulated the vast territories governed by the so-called 'warlords'. An interest in the idea of socialism has started spreading among the Chinese intellectuals in the early 1920s,[8] enhanced by the emancipatory postulates regarding women and workers' rights and calls for the people's self-rule. Mao Zedong and his comrades specifically focused on the conditions of peasantry. In the wartime period of 1931–1949 (spanning from the Japanese invasion of Manchuria to the Liberation), the leaders of the Communist Party of China (CPC) tested the functionality of the new system, underlining the significance of collectivism as a method of living and working, rectification practices, acts of collective as well as individual criticism. Such practices were considered fundamental for the correct organizing of the society as well as for implementing and maintaining the ideologically efficient methods of governance and control.

The transition from the socialist phase to communism was a strategic goal for the leaders and the masses in New China. The campaigns of Great Leap Forward (1958–1962) and Cultural Revolution (1966–1976) were meant to facilitate it. The historians and political science scholars agree in regard to the systemic repressiveness of the Maoist state. Bogdan Góralczyk's words stand representative: "'Communism' was only an official shell; in fact, it was still a classic feudalism and despotism that repudiated opposition and eradicated any attempt of breaking away from the imposed canon" (38). Góralczyk, an internationally acknowledged Polish politologist and diplomat, also notices complexities regarding political valuation of Mao Zedong's rule. Analyzing the figure of the Chairman in a perspective limited to the cult of personality and established apparatus of repression may lead to overlooking the heterogeneity of the Maoist doctrine. Ross Terrill wrote:

> Yet on neither of the two basic tenets of Marxism – a theory of class and a theory of history – was Mao steadily Marxist. In time he may be viewed as a populist dictator with various strands to his thought including anarchism, Confucianism, Marxism, and fascism.
>
> (487)

The culture studies scholars should observe that the doctrine's divergency had a decisive influence on formation of artistic tendencies in New China.

On the following stages of the PRC's development, in its core, the regime relied on ideological convergence of Mao Zedong Thought (*Mao Zedong sixiang*) and Marxism–Leninism adapted accordingly to the Chinese socio-cultural conditions. Such formulated doctrine determined power structure, social and economic organization, formulations and outreach of accepted discourses used in public and private communication as well as the horizon of cognitive, inventive, and critical practices. Among the enduring, ideological assumptions valid in the PRC, one finds a leading role of the CPC and its monopoly over the power apparatus, the principle of the people's dictatorship being performed by the selected (but not commonly voted) group of the Party members, submission of the individual's will and agency to the welfare of the state, privileged position of the military (implying preference for nationalistic attitudes and discourses), and eventually a primacy of political decision making over constituted law which in consequence leads to the acceptance of the methods of mass surveillance and repressive character of the state–citizen relationship. On following stages, these premises were implemented in varied scale and outreach in cultural, economic, and political dimensions of living in the PRC.

Mao authored the texts formative for the New China's ideologists before the PRC was founded but when the revolution was already ongoing (e.g., *On Contradiction*, 1937; *On New Democracy*, 1940; *Talks at the Yan'an Forum of Literature and Art*, 1942). It is necessary to clarify the meaning of the term 'revolution'. According to the studies presented by the multitude of historians, political scientists, and culture scholars, the 'pre-revolutionary' is located before 1911 (the fall of the Qing Dynasty), while the 'Chinese revolution' denotes:

> a long socio-political process (…) that was supposed to start along with Sun Yat-sen rising to power and last continuously until the founding of the PRC, carried out by various 'progressive' and 'patriotic powers' as well as through the efforts of all Chinese people. The term 'revolution' indicates the fact that this process was of distinctively anti-traditionalist features, and its goal was to break away from feudalism and dogmatic, Confucian tradition.
>
> (PAWŁOWSKI 11)

In this sense the cultural period of the 'Chinese Enlightenment' (see Schwarcz, 1986) that symbolically commenced with the 1919 May Fourth Movement (*Wusi yundong*)[9] is addressed as 'revolutionary'. The social order based on feudal traditions began disintegrating under the avalanche of varied, progressive postulates such as democratization and patriotism, socialism and modernization of the means of production, primacy of science, Westernization, facilitation of mass access to schooling, culture, and communication. The progressive social movements quickly absorbed certain politically and ideologically affiliated characteristics: anti-Manchu (anti-Qing), anti-colonial (directed against Euro-Atlantic powers), and anti-Japanese (reacting to the rise of the militarism and imperialism in Japan). In an empowering, discursive attempt to reforge a weakness into strength, the revolted ones demanded breaking away from the 'hundred years of national humiliation' (*bainian guochi*).

The CPC was founded in 1921. Continuity and totality are among the defining features of the Chinese communist revolution. Continuously occurring class struggle is omnipresent in all areas of social life, its aim (attainable in the Maoists' lifetime) is to completely eradicate class differentiation. This kind of intellectual, artistic, but above all military revolution was propagated by the artists and thinkers who, being affiliated or sympathizing with the CPC, in the 1930s and 1940s joined the ranks of the National Salvation Movement (*Jiuwang yundong*).[10]

The communist society accepted the fact that strengthening of the revolutionary consciousness and performance of the revolutionary deeds for the purposes of social and mental liberation as well as masses overtaking power were to be considered primary and daily obligations of any individual within the society. Individuals-masses affirmed this state of things by self-sacrifices and showing enthusiasm. Having complete faith in the doctrine (or affirming having so), they were ready to immediately join the imposed political campaigns. These were the utmost important, operational devices of the social engineering which regulated power relationships.

In the course of the campaigns, the aims, forms, and structures of various social practices and discourses were subjected to thorough redefinition. This implied mass-scale rectification of viewpoints and verification of compliance with the top-down imposed norms and regulations. Frequently, particular cultural facts would give the power apparatus an impulse to launch the campaigns. Along capitalism, the list of Maoist equivalents of Orwellian 'thoughtcrimes' comprised liberalism (e.g., condemned during the 1951 campaign against Sun Yu's film *Life of Wu Xun/Wu Xun Zhuan*), revisionism (in 1961–1965 such allegations were made against the leaders of the ministry of culture, Xia Yan and Chen Huangmei; in 1965 against a prominent historian Wu Han who authored a stage play *Hai Rui Dismissed from Office/Hai Rui baguan*). During the short-term, quasi-thaw Hundred Flowers Campaign (winter of 1956–spring of 1957, *baihuaqifang, baijiazhengming*), the Party's members and working cadres were encouraged to formulate criticism of centrally established regulations and control mechanisms. This unexpectedly genuine movement was stopped fast by enactment of Anti-Rightists Campaign (1957–1959, *fanyou yundong*) when the accusations of liberalism and revisionism were combined with the charges of propagating reactionary feudalism, espionage for the imperialists, and support of the Kuomintang's government in Taiwan. The transition from social criticism of the Hundred Flowers period into political repressions and struggle sessions (mass rallies of public criticism) against the 'rightists' terminated the atmosphere of socialist optimism and decisively reduced the extent of intellectual and artistic freedom.

Managing the society with the means of campaigns that would target particular products of culture, specific individuals, or defined social groups, were complemented with the economic and industrial campaigns aimed at mass mobilization at the cost of individuals' exploitation in terms of material resources as well as physical and mental well-being. One of such dark chapters in the PRC's history was the Great Leap Forward (1958–1962, *da yuejin*). At the highest peak of political tensions, Mao Zedong and his faction launched the 'Great Proletarian Cultural Revolution' (*wenhua dageming*), designed in the name of totality and continuity of revolutionary struggle. In the ideological perspective, the Cultural Revolution embraces the 'continuous revolution theory' (*jixu geming lun*), 'reeducation through work' as well as struggle against feudalism (anti-Confucian), nationalism (anti-Kuomintang), and revisionism (condemnation of the former leaders, Liu Shaoqi and Lin Biao). The Maoist dogma conveyed a conviction of integrity of practice and theory. On the one hand, the communist revolutionaries did not question the validity of their views and methods regardless the extent of brutality of the employed 'necessary means'. On the other, the power apparatus had complete certainty that whenever reformulation of the meanings within the doctrine was needed, the authority of dogma would remain intact. Those unable to keep track and pace, especially the acolytes of former argumentation, would be silenced or 'evaporated'.

In 1968, Franz Schurmann authored a classic study about the Chinese communism. On a general level of understanding ideology, Schurmann acknowledged its twofold character. A 'pure ideology' encompasses 'practical ideology'. Pure ideology of Maoism is referred to as theory (*lilun*), i.e., the selected concepts of Marxism–Leninism applied to the specifically Chinese cultural and historical conditions. Practical ideology of Maoism (thought; *sixiang*) provides a framework for actions that consequently derive from the accepted world view. In the high peak of the 1960s' ideological fervor, Schurmann argued:

> Mao's creation of thought is a continuing process without any foreseeable conclusion. Unification of theory and practice continues, adding to thought. The new revolutionary generation is instructed to do more than read the thought of Mao Tse-tung. It is urged to use it as a model for combining theory and practice, and so develop an outlook in which ideology becomes a central part of every-day living and working.
>
> (29–30)

He described the relationship between *lilun* and *sixiang* as an equation where theory (truths of Marxism–Leninism) plus practice (practice of revolution and construction in China) equals thought (the Thought of Mao Tse-tung) (see 30).

The Chinese system manifests an iron consistency in consolidating its apparatus along the line defined in the course of communist revolution, while at the same time it is constantly capable to remold and redesign the very same line in accordance with the requirements imposed by the current socio-political reality in its local as well as global aspect. Since its founding, the New China has undergone numerous and thorough renovations but the fundament built upon the Mao Zedong Thought turned out well firm, and the construction spans applied in it are perfectly flexible and carrying. Any necessary modifications implemented at any later stage do not ruin the integrity of key terms of the revolution – party-state democracy is a function of the people's dictatorship performed for the welfare of the nation, for the sake of class struggle, and for the purpose of reasserting Chinese cultural supremacy.

OBSERVING CHINESE ANIMATION FROM THE DISTANCE

Noël Burch's famous study on Japanese cinema opens with a quotation from Ki No Tsurayaki "To the distant observer / They are chatting of the blossoms / Yet in spite of appearances / Deep in their hearts / They are thinking very different thoughts." This notion relates *per analogiam* to the research on China presented by any non-native to Chinese cultures. 'Distant observation' requires realizing and accepting the limits of intercultural understanding – regardless of how rigidly one defines the object of reflection and applied methods, the aim of presenting a fully exhaustive account of discussed phenomena lies beyond the 'observer's' capacities. Ignoring this constraint, even if unwillingly, may lead to megalomania, naivety, or appropriation.

The general objective here lies in the reconstruction of the dynamics of political and cultural processes wherein the forms of Chinese animation have crystallized and become closely integrated with an extremely anti-individualist power apparatus. Necessarily, the overall concern is reduced to more specific questions that derive from the idiosyncratic character of source material and depart from such features of symbolic communication which are comprehensible 'beyond reasonable doubt' to any viewer. The employed interdisciplinary mode of the research interweaves perspectives of film and animation studies with the reflection grounded in broader disciplines of cultural studies (popular culture, propaganda) as well as the history of idea, political science, and anthropology. The problem of historical specifics of ideologization of the artistic process remains at the center of reflection. Socio-political concepts and analytical devices organizing the approach of ideological criticism allow one to effectively examine selected material as manifestations of two major aims bestowed on cinema production apparatus in Maoist China: popularization of the remolded cultural heritage and establishment of new forms of indoctrinatory entertainment.

In order not to ramify this discussion over the necessary extent, the assumed understanding of 'propaganda' follows the classic concept of Jacques Ellul (1973[1975]) who saw it as an institutional and psychological action of mobilizing people through reinforcing their views and beliefs while masking the intensions of the apparatus that produces propagandistic discourses. As a specific technique of social engineering, it can be characterized as being driven by effectiveness principle, synced with education, and possessing highly ambivalent relationship with truth. The scope, depth, and coherence of propaganda should be examined when asking questions about means and extent of its outreach. As numerous propaganda scholars observed (most notably, Chomsky and Herman, 2008), propagandistic communication (of inherently mass character) does not require the function of a full-scale, punitive, *post factum* control as its prerequisite mechanisms can be found in self-censorship and preventive censorship.

Animation is treated here as a modality of the film medium; thus, the concerns of high importance for the film scholars are revoked – above all, the question of realism in cinema. At the same time, this study looks at the animated film as historical evidence where ideologized practices of dominant doctrine residue. In order to simultaneously accommodate both perspectives, animation has to be perceived as an element of visual culture, i.e., as an object in a historicized, visual environment explained by Tang Xiaobing[11] as following:

> Most of these visual objects are studied in academic disciplines such as art history and film studies, but I believe the notion of visual culture allows us to appreciate their significance in more interactive and more explanatory contexts. More than embodying a specific artistic imagination or conceptual innovation, these works of art take up different positions (…) in an evolving structure of visibility (…) They illustrate a succession of changing practices and paradigms. (…) resonance of continuing efforts to create a distinct Chinese culture and identity in the modern era.
>
> (2)

Uncovering a position of the animated film in the architecture of the Maoist visual culture begins with acknowledging two determinants of Chinese culture production, i.e., *gaizao* and *guoqing*. The first is a strategy of remolding (reformulating, adapting to the new conditions) such symbolic forms and contents derived from the Chinese cultural heritage that are substantial for the collective identity-building processes. The process of ideologization is of particular dynamic: revolutionary elements of the doctrine are grounded in the widely understandable specifics of the Chinese civilization's historical and cultural conditions (*guoqing*) but the 'inherited' elements (essentially contradicting the idea of a total revolution that fiercely renounces the past) are 'filtered' through the doctrine, subjected to new (re)interpretations or thorough, semantic revisions and interferences. These two significant operational concepts condition the use of metaphors and symbols related to the past traditions in the openly propagandistic communication. An ideologized concern of integrating any given film with the revolutionary China's reality was a crucial (required, constructive, and meaning making) strategy of the Maoist visual culture.

Since Mao Zedong's 1942 'Yan'an lectures', the Chinese artists and intellectuals were bound by the 'art for the masses' principle. Thematically and aesthetically the purpose of art creation in New China was to serve the people, portray their living conditions, and illuminate the 'real life' as the only valuable source of inspiration.[12] Stefan Landsberger outlined the arts' systemic function in Maoist view:

> Art should unite and educate the people, inspire the struggle of revolutionary people and eliminate the bourgeoisie. Art had to be revolutionized and guided by Mao Zedong Thought, its contents had to be militant and reflect 'real life'. Proletarian ideology, Communist morale and spirit, revolutionary heroism were the messages of this new type of hyper-realistic, politicized art that took precedence over style and technique and that differed in many aspects from art in the preceding years.
>
> (147)

The debates and findings of culture, film, and visual art scholars[13] regarding the concept of realism in Maoist artistic practice establish analytical framework for the discussion about realism in Chinese animated propaganda of the 1940s–1970s. One notices that the category of 'Chinese classic cinema' proposed by Chris Berry (22–24) adequately applies to the SAFS *modus operandi* (maintained up until the late 1980s). The animated production was highly stable in its institutional dimension (SAFS as an exclusive producer; distribution centrally planned and limited in regard to the foreign circulation) as well as discursive one (production subjected to the demands of propaganda, entertainment, and education). The analyses of *The Emperor's Dream* and *Wanderings of Sanmao* outline aesthetic relationships between animation and pre-1949 critical realism of the left-wing artistic tendencies (specifically significant in the history of cinema, cartoon, and caricature – *manhua*), while the chapters regarding the films made by 'hardline' director You Lei (*Rooster Crows at Midnight*, *The Little 8th Route Army*) revolve around the manifestations of revolutionary, romanticist, and model realism in animation.

Marc Ferro emphasized film status as history, finding film to be a document attesting to the truths about political and cultural reality of the society whose institutions produced a given film. Even if the document is distorted and manipulated (e.g., being propaganda work), the film medium preserves potency to "destroy alter image" (29). A viewer (particular historian) activates this potency by critically analyzing the film. In this sense, the films co-create historical events and reproduce current patterns of historical understanding. Film analysis is a path to revise the mechanisms of how history (structures rather than events) is narrated and understood (to become "interested in invisible, permanent structures and in transformations, realizing that, over a long time span, structures partially eclipse events", Ferro 28). A film experience – creative act, institutionalized production, critical reception – enable the eclipse of reality. All three aspects inform on historical conditions of the moment when the film was realized and indicate the patterns of how the collectives historicize their current social, political, and cultural identifications.

The discussion about the films is a conversation about the relationship between the art and the society that produces it. The bilateral nature of this exchange (see Greenblatt 1987) reveals itself when the specific situations are critically examined (e.g., propaganda discourses, strategies of representation, reception, and canon-building practices) as well as in the reconnaissance of the established structures that determine the dynamics and outreach of these manifestations. One acknowledges here the echoes of the French ideological criticism. Revoking its arguments, it is necessary to raise a certain admonition. The politics of representation postulated by the circle of *Cahiers du Cinéma* in 1969–1972 served the purpose of establishing analytical apparatus focused on capitalist film production that was criticized and commented by the radical opponents of this system who were nevertheless speaking from inside of it. Sadly, these cinephiles fascinated with Maoism did not make efforts to verify the operative mechanisms of the cinema subjected to the dogma of a continuous revolution. A direct transposition of the French film criticism to the discussion on Maoist cinema is pointless as the latter did never hide intellectual and aesthetic unity of the film and dominant ideology, whereas the French theoreticians sought to unveil ideological mystifications in the films. Their debates may be however inspirational in regard to the methods of identifying the wide production structure as ideological as well as to the discussion on long-term ideological effects generated by the cinema.

Jean-Luc Comolli and Paul Narboni argued:

> A film which has not examined its place in the relations of production, the economic-cultural status of conditions and means of its specific practice (…) can do nothing other than reproduce both the economic norms and cultural norms of production, and thus, in the moment of its fabrication, can only reduplicate the modes of formulation/inculcation of the dominant ideology.
>
> (171)

Maoist cinema, as a production apparatus, was created and controlled by the official institutions and it openly affirmed the imposed, indoctrinating agenda. The filmmakers were not supposed to determine the character of the relationship between their art and the dominant system. As a principle, they followed the system by reproducing binding codes, symbols, and aesthetics. The New China's cinema was (literally) born during the midst of war; thus, in the bilateral relationship with the viewers, it has positioned itself as a device stimulating patriotic and communist morale. The means of production acquired after the evacuating Japanese or Kuomintang studios symbolically functioned as war trophies. These specific 'genetic conditions' were sustained with the production policies heavily relying on propaganda technique (see Wain, 2009).

Noticing the above does not mean that the Chinese filmmakers, who have complied with the dominant doctrine, did not foster the reflection on the film art's ideological position. On the contrary, in the course of required and expected criticism and self-criticism practices, this concern appeared central. Ideologization of the art negated (or even condemned) artistic individualism, but at the same time, this process justified explorations of purely artistic or technical filmmaking aspects. Sean Macdonald summarizes in detail the discussion about the definition and function of animation within the Maoist culture production system held in 1960 (Macdonald 105–114). Animators and other culture creators debated artistic qualities of the just-emerging *minzu* style, animation's disposition to convey fantasy, and its ideological usefulness and consistency with the doctrine. Under such conditions, the animators validated expressive qualities of surrealism, nostalgia, magical fairytales; such were the conditions that You Lei affirmed with daring and unconventional use of cinematography and editing.

Jean-Patrick Lebel who polemized with the *Cahier du Cinéma* authors by defying inherently ideological origins of cinema, discussed the 'ideological effects' that generate images of reality, remain subjected to the dominant system, and which are also present at all stages of film production and reception. The film's overall ideological effect is a sum of all such determinants that resurrect, confluence, and interchange one another in order to procure a film's holistic meaning on the ideological plane (see Lebel 1971). The emerged patterns organize the reflection, communication, and reception of visual, narrative, and performative symbols; they are capable of reducing complex, ideological, discursive contents to universal and unquestionable icons, gestures, and myths. The Maoist cinema (live-action and animation) appears as a laboratory of culture production where the ideological effects became 'overheated'. Reforging the pivotal, social emotions into petrified, ritualized forms of manipulated communication led the filmmakers to the limits of creating convincing and emotive, realistic works.

Ideological dimension of the Maoist animated production is verified against the source literature, i.e., relevant writings of Mao Zedong and Jiang Qing. Interestingly, the Mao Zedong Thought has never been presented in the form of a singular and binding thesis. *Red Book* (*Mao Zhuxi Yulu*), edited by Lin Biao in 1964, is composed of selected quotations from the Chairman. Extensive 'collected works' do not encompass all numerous directives, speeches and lectures, letters to the cadres, etc., which have played a significant role in formulating the twists and revisions of doctrine at particular stages of the China's political history – the doctrine itself was subjected to the continuous process of remolding. Dogma that has remained stable in spite of the doctrine's general changeability considers the organization of the world as radically polarized (class struggle, theory of contradiction). The analyses of particular events and phenomena or instructions regarding daily life conduct were frequently updated and corrected. Maoist discourses of arts and criticism unveil tensions erupting from necessity of anticipating the new, forthcoming interpretations of the doctrine and requirement to affirm, resound, and petrify the patterns formerly established within it.

The meanings generated by the practical ideology that are manifested in the Maoist animated propaganda are examined in the light of contexts of political and cultural history. Dominick LaCapra notes: "Contextualization is necessary for historical understanding" (17). He acknowledged this method as highly significant in the process of integrating historical research with the problems of experience, trauma, and microhistory. Contextualization has a potency to explicate historical occurrences as it forces the researchers to restrain from formulating fixed hypotheses regarding the groundbreaking and unique character of the discussed events, facts, and texts. Creating a map of interdependencies allows one to locate filmmaking practice as an element of the social system (maintaining or questioning its organizing principles), dependent on influences deriving from the transformations of political, economic, cultural, and technological character. LaCapra warns the readers: "But as an exclusive mode of explanation or when taken to the extreme of overcontextualization that excludes responsive understanding, it becomes dubious" (Ibid.), and so this method, applied extensively in this research, serves only the purpose of exposing cultural references under the condition their analysis complements and dialogues with the studied problems. The correlated network of culture production manifests the dynamics of the negotiations regarding meanings, identities, and valuation that at the same time involve problems of artistic expression, dominant doctrine, and functioning of the mass society who kept defining their own subjectivity in a continuous process, repeated and revised over again.

Four selected films are submitted to critical, contextual analysis in order to trace the remolding practices of Maoist culture apparatus in constructing the founding story of the Liberation and establishment of the New China accordingly to the changeable interpretations of the dominant doctrine. In 1947–1973, in order to solidify relationship between the animation and its viewers, the revolutionary puppet film's aesthetics and its narrative backbone kept undergoing substantial modifications but arrived at forms commonly considered to be detached from the real life's values. The history of Chinese animated propaganda – a microhistory of Chinese visual culture – sustains observations of Elizabeth Perry, an art historian, who noted:

> The idea of a revolutionary tradition is inherently ironic. Revolutions are intended to overthrow traditions, not enshrine them. Yet nation-states born of revolution construct myths about their historical origins and political legacies that prove as powerful and persistent as they are contradictory and contested.
>
> (1)

ENGLISH-LANGUAGE NARRATIVES OF CHINESE ANIMATION HISTORY[14]

By the time when the Chinese independent animation wave started, the English-language scholarship discussing problems of the Chinese animation history was in short supply. Few chapters in the monographs and articles (Ehrlich and Jin, 2001; Wu, 2009; Lent and Xu, 2010) served as basic introduction to this vast and complex area, posing significant questions but not delivering satisfying answers due to their short-length format. The readers interested in discovering trends, tendencies, and approaches of the animators in Mao and Deng eras could have also turned to the pioneering works written by the European animated film curators: Swiss animated film critic Bruno Edera (1980) and French curator Marie-Claire Quiquemelle (1991). Film scholars such as Jay Leyda (1972), Stephen Teo (2009), Mary Farqhuar, and Chris Berry (2005) referred to animation as one of the devices functioning in the mechanisms of the visual culture but did not study thoroughly the animated film's historical development. A similar approach can be found in the writings and popularization activities of Christopher Rea (2021; curated YouTube channel 'Modern Chinese Cultural Studies'). Rolf Giesen's (2015) filmography of

Chinese animation in 1922–2012 attempts to account for all films produced in the period but this publication is not free from certain factual inaccuracies.

Arguably novel quality was manifested in Sean Macdonald's study *Animation in China* (2016), a highly important reference for the author of this publication. Macdonald adheres to the principle of historicization (early in the book he poses a significant statement: "Although this is changing, historically Chinese animation media has been particularized as nationally and ethnically specific", 4) and acknowledges various ideologically meaningful, intellectual, and aesthetic operations employed throughout the decades by the Chinese animators:

> The model is the teleology of visual culture within which many classics of SAFS animation were produced. (…) During a period when the cartoon became the dominant form of realist representation, animation was another form of image repetition, another form of simulacrum. The model represented a frame that determined stylization in figural representation, and in the representation of conflict.
>
> (13)

Macdonald analyzes three famous feature-length films[15] and considers the problems of ideological/meaning-making disposition of cinematic expression that elevated artistic quality of these productions. Activities that characterize SAFS outputs such as creating propaganda, conducting theoretical debates on realism and fantasy, preserving ambiguous qualities of caricature and irony are perceived by Macdonald as aspects of creative and critical discourses that enabled representation of "authentic images about an absent reality" (Epstein 95, qtd. in Macdonald 10). At the same time, he remains aware of the trap related to the historicization perspective, i.e., the researchers' inclination to narrate their reflection on China with the use of Western-oriented conventions of the so-called Chinese area studies. Focus on the textual tissue of culture texts, relations of intertextuality, and problems of serialization of the culture production in the socialist period helps Macdonald to avoid it.

In 2017, John A. Lent and Xu Ying substantially expanded their long-lasting, comparative investigations into relationship between comics and animation. Discussing *manhua* and animation simultaneously appears perfectly validated – the researchers emphasize the fact that the first cadres of the Northeast Film Studio in Changchun (the predecessor of the SAFS) recruited from the circles of the graphic and caricature artists. Lent and Xu examine stylistic, intertextual, and ideological correlations determining development patterns of both these aspects of visual culture. They acknowledge specificity of animated film as an autonomous artistic medium relying on source material analyses (films and documentation of production) and interviews with the animators. An attempt in mapping wide, common symbolic structures complements the reflection on relationship between popular culture and society.

In the most recent years, the Hong Kong-based Association for Chinese Animation Studies (ACAS) intensified its activities to stimulate networking of the international community of Chinese animation researchers. A massive Inaugural Conference of ACAS was held in 2021, the event held online in the span of three months gathered almost seventy speakers who presented multilayered discussions on history and contemporaneity of Chinese animated cinemas. Daisy Yan Du's (ACAS' *spiritus movens*) contributions to the discipline have substantially relocated the leading concerns of the contemporary scholarship in the discipline. Above all, Du observes that Chinese animation has been continuously developed in a mode of artistic, transnational confluence. Carefully studying artists and films' mobility, interpersonal exchanges, and creative influences within Asia and beyond, she relates such 'flows of culture' to the specificities of medium (flexibility, fluidity, evanescence, etc.). Du's inspiring research method is to converse and learn from the 'actants' of the past film production and to rely on oral history testimonies as well as interviews (written texts or videos).[16] Both these approaches inspire the author of the presented book in her currently ongoing work dedicated to the concerns of Sino-European opening up at the animated film festivals in the 1980s. The release of Du's major publications (monograph *Animated Encounters*, 2019; edited collective volume *Chinese Animation and Socialism*, 2022) overlapped with the preparations of this book. The differences between the author and Du's approaches towards certain categories should be explained.

The presented book refers to the discussed period of the 1940s–1970s as the 'Maoist era' and, in consequence, it speaks of 'Maoist animation'. In her both publications, Du predominantly uses the term 'socialist animation' ("Defined strictly, socialist animation refers to the animated films produced between the late 1940s and the late 1970s. Defined loosely, it means the animated films made between the late 1940s and the early 1990s", *Chinese Animation and Socialism*, 3). The here-assumed term 'Maoist' emphasizes understanding of animation as an expression of this particular doctrine (communicated with the use of a specific, audiovisual language). The wider, institutional, societal, and artistic dimensions of animated filmmaking, however acknowledged here, remain of secondary importance. Du's authorial monograph challenges

> the reified myth that art and literature during the Mao era were no more than political propaganda that slavishly served the government. (…) According to conventional studies of Chinese cinema, it was only with the rise of the fifth-generation filmmakers in the 1980s that the totalitarian and didactic cinema witnessed a breakthrough in terms of artistic style and content – an innovation and

> elevation enabled, in part, by the transnational mobility and popularity of these films.
>
> (3–2)

A surplus of scholarship discussing the output and influence of the 'fifth generation'[17] indeed contributes to such generalized view. Nevertheless, one may find a quantitively and qualitatively significant English-language output delivered by various researchers who account for diversity of the themes and styles of filmmaking during the Maoist era and who at the same time maintain critical perspective on film art as a politicized device of communication between the viewers and the state which owned the means of production and distribution (see Marchetti, 1997; Hemelryk Donald and Voci, 2008; McGrath, 2010; Pickowicz, 2012; Teo, 2013; Wang, 2017). Furthermore, this notion appears rather related to the scholarship centered on the concerns of live-action filmmaking, while the animation studies available in English language seems to be almost exclusively focused on the concepts of fine art film (*meishu donghua pian*), national style (*minzu*), intertextuality or genetic kinship between animation and *manhua*. Majority of the animation study publications condense the problems of political history to the necessary 'setting', a background that allows to anchor the reflection on animation in time and space but rarely constitutes core reference of the presented analyses.[18]

One cannot disagree with one of Du's introductory assertions: "It comes as no surprise that many animated films with great artistic value were distanced, if not completely divorced, from totalitarian politics during the socialist era" (Du 4). The presented research deliberately leaves the question of artistic values aside. The films discussed here either openly pronounce their ideological function (*The Emperor's Dream*; *The Little 8th Route Army*) or they are adapted from heavily politicized source texts (*The Wanderings of Sanmao*; *The Rooster Crows at Midnight*) – to contextualize them in terms of Maoist doctrine's discourse is to account for the ideological material they were built upon. When Du discusses propagandistic works, she emphasizes their reception among the Chinese audiences; such concerns exceed the scope of the reflection presented here. This book rather upholds to the idea that studying past propaganda mechanisms contributes to the multifaceted understanding of phenomena occurring contemporarily. The presented analyses aim at chartering discursive features of Maoist animation which – just as the past artistic inventions and fine art techniques – keep stimulating contemporary filmmakers to comment and criticize, revise and restructure their native animated cinematography traditions in order to come up with utmost surprising, complex, and ambivalent works. Furthermore, when exceeding the boundaries of national (animated) cinema and looking at Chinese animation as a specific but one of many nexuses in global film history and theory, one acknowledges it as uniquely consistent in serving the government as a device of indoctrination – however, not in a slavish manner, but rather in a way of affirming animated film's creative potential and dedicating it at the power's disposal. Whenever (and wherever) such phenomenon occurs, those inclined to learn from global history of culture, should not look away.

MINZU STYLE: A CONDENSED VIEW

Examinations of the national (*minzu*) style in animation remain a core concern of the majority of scholarly publications discussing Chinese animation traditions. This book consciously resigns from participating in this ramified debate since it focuses on openly agitating works of animated propaganda. The author's understanding of *minzu* should be nevertheless explicated as the context of the national film art will be reoccurring at points.

Minzu style animation appears as an artistic phenomenon manifesting characteristics of traditional Chinese culture and it is conceptualized in regard to the specific socio-political, historical circumstances when the representative films were made,[19] and – importantly – when the distinctive features of the style became defined ('sanctioned') by the artists. The established periodization of *minzu* style divides its development in 'two golden eras' – the first one of 1957–1964, when the groundbreaking technical and aesthetic innovations (above all, ink-and-wash painting animation, *shuimo donghua*) were conceptualized and exercised by the SAFS filmmakers (among them notably Duan Xiaoxuan, Qian Yunda, Yan Dingxian, Lin Wenxiao, Tang Cheng, Qian Jiajun, Jin Xi, Wan Laiming, Te Wei), and the second one of 1979–1992, when the *minzu* themes and motifs became re-envisioned in the spirit of the 1980s modernization tendencies (films of Ma Kexuan, Zhou Keqin, Hu Xionghua, Hu Jinqing).

On the most basic level, the 'national style' denotes those films whose material (technique, art, and sound design) expose forms of traditional expression (e.g., ink wash painting, Chinese cut-out and shadow theater, Beijing opera).[20] Another general level of conceptualizing *minzu* (frequently encountered in online, fandom communication) simply refers to the 'classics', i.e., historical heritage of Chinese animated cinematography (films made at the SAFS until the end of the 1980s), their contemporary remakes, and original productions employing traditional conventions.[21]

In their expanded study from 2017, John A. Lent and Xu Ying present more nuanced perspective on relevant meanings of *minzu*. While the technical advancement and strategies of cultural heritage adaptation (remolding) continue to determine line of historical development, they turn the readers' attention to the concern of cultural and political conditions impacting the production. They are also interested in personal, individual life stories of the animators. Discussing the 'golden era', they diagnose structure and dynamics of the SAFS' *milieu* where *minzu* style thrived: government's investments in animated film studio, "good atmosphere" between the cadres based on master–apprentice relationships that stimulated creative approaches towards challenges imposed by the leaders in the spirit of inventiveness and experimentation (162–172). Also, Daisy Yan Du considers *minzu* to be a more multifaceted phenomenon. She emphasizes plurality and writes of the national styles instead of a style. Furthermore, she notes:

> I use national style and national identity to refer to this institutionalized discourse that originated in the late 1950s and was revived during the 1980s to dominate animated filmmaking and academic studies. (…) national style changes as the Chinese society changes.
>
> (17)

A simplified story of the *minzu* style origins at SAFS[22] has it that Te Wei, the studio's long-term artistic director and former *manhua* artist, on the verge of 1956 and 1957 raised a slogan "Road to *minzu* style" (see Macdonald 92) as a response to the increasing, top-down imposed demands to significantly differentiate revolutionary China's cinema from other countries' film production (specifically, the USSR and the United States). Naturally the process of arriving at a national form was much more complex. The thoroughly studied context of the emergence of socialist, national style in fine arts gives an idea of how many theoretical debates and ideological controversies were involved in the process (among them, the discussion about Qi Baishi, the master of traditional painting, whose art was first defied by the 'hard-liners' but who has eventually regained widespread appreciation since mid-1950s; his works directly inspired first *shuimo donghua* film *Where Is Mama?*, 1960). In the breakthrough 1957, Ai Qing advocated reforms of national painting art acknowledging inherent contradictions of such task:

> I have heard that some people dislike the word 'remoulding' [*gaizao*]. They prefer instead to be perpetually imprisoned by the bonds of plagiarism and imitation. (…) The government rewards Qi Baishi for precisely this sort of

> creative labor. His great achievements in art require diligent and systematic research in the future.
>
> (AI 7–9, QTD. IN ANDREWS 113–115)

SAFS was not a deserted island but well-invested and highly promising (in regard to talents involved as cadres and significant, ideological status of target audience – youth and children) 'factory' bestowed with important tasks. Dilemmas in conceptualizing the meanings, contents, and forms of national style created with the means of a given medium have not bypassed the animators.

Both Wu Weihua and Sean Macdonald discuss *minzu* in reference to *meishu* (fine arts). Wu noticed the problem of semantic exploitation of the category of *minzu* and *meishu* in international film studies:

> The conceptualization of *minzu* and the constitution of *meishu* are more like modern catachreses emerging at a given moment as a mutation that produces a language of its own (…), by deconstructing tradition and normative formation that were nurtured by the non-socialist others. I argue that the *meishu* film-related catachresis is a discourse-based cultural subversion rather than a linguistic revision. (…) In a broader sense, this conceptualization connects with socialist ideology and aesthetic escape, compromise and creative practices of Chinese animators in dealing with state discourse and in diversifying visual characteristics.
>
> (32–33)

He points out that the non-Chinese researchers unavoidably misrecognize certain ideological and cultural meanings by overlooking fluidity of the definitions and theoretical concepts created by Chinese animation production and criticism apparatus (e.g., individualized relationship between author, production system, and viewers' expectations). Wu conceptualizes *minzu* as a capacious set of references and discourses aiding the individual to endure the demands of the socialist culture and politics. Artistic, *meishu* film is a traditionalist form which mediates meanings of *minzu* (national/ethnic) style.

It is however difficult to disagree with Sean Macdonald when he indicates certain redundancy of Wu's argumentation: "National style is very much a process, but the cultural production that emerged alongside national style discourse cannot be simply viewed within the frame of national style" (82). Departing from Wan Laiming's notion that the fine art film was a revolutionary aim of the Chinese animators, Macdonald suggests to apply the category of *minzu* to those productions which not only borrow traditional conventions and discursive motifs from the symbolic reservoir of Chinese civilization, but above all which function as variations of historical, artistic expression. It can be said that Macdonald searches for *minzu* in films that work as contact points between the expression found in a tissue of traditional culture and the one that results from remolding of the heritage in the spirit of accepted, ideological methods of recognition, understanding, and interpretation. He perceives *meishu* films (category he relates to institutional practice, training, education, and craftmanship) as a perfect example of *minzu* style tendency. *Minzu* film can be of artistic character but its prime function is to produce ideological meanings and this 'obligation' results from the function designed for the cinema apparatus in the nation-building process.

From the perspective of film studies, the reflection on *minzu* outlines the Chinese artists' innovativeness in the use of film language employed for the purpose of transposing traditional imageries and narratives. However, a multilayered understanding of *minzu* exceeds purely theoretical deliberations about film art. There are at least two more planes of reflection capable of explaining the pertinence of this category. Firstly, *minzu* encompasses a variety of meanings sedimented over the term throughout the centuries. The term 'nation' refers to frequently dramatic, philosophical, and political discussions that established both cultural and ideological identity of the mainland China's society in the 20th century. Under none latitude, the category of 'nation' remains neutral as it evokes reflection on immanent civilizational values, nationalism, and hierarchical relations between the groups functioning within the societies organized as political entities (the state); thus, it requires consideration regarding the status of the national and ethnic minorities within it. As soon as a label of 'national' appears, the question of 'extra-national' surges. Thus, *minzu* style suggests reading of animated films as records of auto-images of Chinese nationals and their cultures. Critical analysis of such films implies posing questions regarding entities who are missing in the greater picture, the reasons for particular groups to be portrayed as external or internal enemies, the character of symbolic and discursive means that convey the notion of a transparent, unquestionable, national unity, etc. Eventually, the discussion on *minzu* attests to the potency of *soft power* of animated film and emphasizes the filmmakers' understanding that the cultural, Chinese specificity manifested in the films can be used as tools for resisting cultural interferences (depending on historical context, one may comparatively discuss Chinese and Soviet, American, Japanese, Korean cultures, etc.) as much as devices used for reclaiming and strengthening one's own cultural identity in the process of symbolic confrontation with others.

THE FOUNDING MYTH

In the canonical narratives of the Chinese animated cinema, its history began in 1957 when the formal establishment of SAFS was concluded and the animators entered the road to *minzu* style. In other words, animation as a form of cinematic expression obtained institutional autonomy, production resources, methods of persuasion, and formal devices which allowed the animators to convey the spirit, needs, and values of the Chinese nation. This situation, however rooted in factual grounds, can be also treated as a manifestation of a particular film history myth. The national style (*minzu*) has been crystallizing in the animators' minds and inside the studio ateliers for years – or even decades, while its mature forms were to be appreciated by the spectators only briefly before the Cultural Revolution (1966).

In accordance with this widespread view, the narration of the Chinese animation history appears linear and progressive, and its following phases of the development are marked with strong contours. However, if the researchers allow the boundaries to blur, they will discover that historically, the SAFS production has revealed a characteristic of recurrences of particular themes, tropes, motifs, and symbols. At the same time, the aim of delivering ideological communication required the filmmakers to resolve tensions between unambiguity of the doctrine's formulations and animation's inherent, subjectifying specifics (above all, transformational nature of images and associative potential of narrative).

On October 1, 1949, Mao Zedong proclaimed the rise of the New China performing a breakthrough political gesture. Recorded with the movie camera, this moment became a globally resonating scene in the myth-building network of images. Nevertheless, the patterns of the new socialist, Chinese culture had been formulated prior to this event. Attempting to indicate a concrete 'point zero' when its fundaments were established seems futile. In a mode characteristic for the Chinese civilization, the socialist philosophy and expression have been emerging from the sedimentation of traditional values, foreign influences, and grassroots willingness of the members of the society to internalize the newly appearing currents. Several events of a 'milestone' status should be nonetheless recalled: release of the first issue of *New Youth* (September 1915),[23] May Fourth Movement (1919), literary output of Lu Xun (1881–1936), rapid development of press in the 1920s and the 1930s (see Fairbank and Goldman 2006); trend of social, critical realism in the cinema of the 1930s (see Shen 2005); militant mobilization of the artists in the National Salvation Movement; Mao Zedong's 'Yan'an talks' of 1942 in which he indicated the direction of ideological and aesthetic development of literature, film, theater, etc. These events charted the grounds for intense and frequently dramatic debates about aesthetics, aims of artistic creativity, world views, and ethics of the artists themselves.[24]

At the beginning of the 20th century, the Chinese society has faced the necessity of reorganization of the social order in its domestic dimension (the fall of the Qing Empire, bankruptcy of the Republican ideas) as well as international one (Chinese nation's submission to the foreign imperial powers, Japanese invasion). The sinicized Marxism formulated by the thinkers such as Chen Duxiu (1879–1942), Li Dazhao (1889–1927), Qu Qiubai (1899–1935), Mao Zedong, and Liu Shaoqi appeared as one of numerous possible answers to the ongoing crises experienced at that time by the Chinese society. In the course of the decades, this answer turned out the victorious one. A completeness of an ideological victory is inseparable from the narrative potency of the culture. Not only a triumphant doctrine regulates spheres of politics and social organization, but it also holistically influences the strategies of storytelling and mechanisms of understanding history in its macro- and micro-dimension. In the most universal sense, this potency of a doctrine was discussed by Leszek Kołakowski: "A mythical organization of the world (that is, the rules of understanding empirical realities as meaningful) is permanently present in culture. (…) Myth degenerated when it changed into a doctrine, that is, a product demanding and seeking proof" (3); moreover, the Polish philosopher claimed that a need to believe in the continuity of humans' values and a need to perceive the world as a continuous entity are equally significant in maintaining the mythical order in culture-building processes.

A mythical world order shapes the story of *genesis*. The individuals, but also the groups, who seek to consolidate their own identity and to affirm their right to historical heritage (as long as they prove to be worthy of it), find fundamental meanings in the narrative of origin. Founding myths of all communities, and especially of those living under totalitarian rule, become highly significant toposes of artistic creativity. Cultural reinterpretations of an ideological *genesis* neutralize current problems and needs, uplift historical memory, and when the groups become a subject of an attack, these stories unify them in an act of the myth's defense. In the view of decision makers of the Maoist culture production, animated films were to ideologically educate the youth. It was only natural for the animation filmmakers to search narrative inspirations for their works in the history of the newly formed party-state. Again, only naturally they were inclined to emphasize such contents of the doctrine that could best fit the needs of ideologically correct forms of development and socialization of the youngest generation. Additionally, and importantly, such contents had to be immune from devaluation. This last objective may be considered the most difficult to properly execute since the Maoist doctrine is characterized as constantly changeable. Its formulations and structures were dependent on the political will of one man and correlated with his shifting position and power performance on the political arena. Considering this context, it seems probable that animated film directors and script writers' focus on the theme of the PRC's founding myth to some extent might have been a conscious decision of both ideological and existential nature. A story of the moment when 'the time began', validated by glorification, martyrology, and victory rhetoric, cannot be easily questioned; hence, it remains a relative safe zone for imaginative, creative work under totalitarian conditions.

The process of establishment and overtaking power by the Communist Party of China lasted almost through three decades. The first Party's unit was formally established on July 1, 1921 in Shanghai, and throughout its initial years, it had relied on an engagement of a narrow circle of domestic activists and party-organizing work of the emigrants based in Japan and Europe. The 1920s were turbulent times for the communists, this decade was marked with changing trajectory of the alliances with the ruling (over the majority of Chinese territory) National Party (KMT) led by Chiang Kai-shek. Held in a political and strategic defense, in 1934 the communists began evacuation to the north where in Yan'an (Shaanxi province) they have formed their famous bases. The wartime wanderings lasted until 1935; named as the Long March (*changzheng*), this event absorbed great significance in the revolutionary historiography:

> The myth was born, and it remains the enduring emblem of China today. We can hardly escape it. The Long March was enshrined for the nation in the musical extravaganzas *East Is Red* and *Ode to the Long March*, and feature films of battles during the March became cinema classics. They took the idealism, optimism and heroism of the Long Marchers and imprinted them on our minds. The myth glowed ever brighter with the help of two major adulatory accounts, both, oddly, by Americans: Edgar Snow's *Red Star over China*, in 1936, and Harrison Salisbury's *Long March: The Untold Stories*, in 1985. With the imprimatur of the Chinese Communist Party, they made the myth close to impregnable.
>
> (SUN, *THE LONG MARCH* 1–2)

Mass glorification of the Long March in official propaganda eventually generated various deconstruction attempts with the means of critical historical studies.[25] The Long March is continuously perceived as a founding myth of the CPC by its proponents, revisionists as well as the regime's opponents.

When one accepts this assumption, the Chinese animated film history appears even more complex and ambiguous for the myth of the Long March is not an important narrative storyline in the films made at the SAFS. 1930s' retreat under pressure from Kuomintang or building the bases in the caves of Yan'an have not found its imagery in any of the acknowledged SAFS' productions of the period. The animated worlds created in Shanghai praise the People's Liberation Army (PLA), its soldiers (and especially the divisions of the famous 8th Route Army), and supporting masses. The specific strategy of telling the CPC's founding myth in animated film relied on negating the mythical story's status as a singular, concrete event (e.g., Long March) and transferring an aura of *genesis* into series of smaller events, typical for the wartime period, nevertheless deprived of references to any particular, factual, and unique event or actions of an individual, heroic character.

The themes of 'war with Japanese' and 'war with Kuomintang' became autonomous, self-sufficient, and self-instigating reservoirs of symbols and narrative structures capable of sustaining the founding myth of the People's Republic of China. The world presented in puppet animated war films is inhabited by simple and suffering people who finally defied the oppressors while awaiting the communist army's arrival. In this world, the time stretches from 1931 to 1949; thus, the Japanese, American, and Chinese nationalists belong to one, unified group of villains. It is the final moment of oppression and the beginning of national salvation. Importantly, as much as the 8th Route's Army's victory is certain and necessary, the narrative axis exposes the people's preparations for the Liberation. The masses perform their agency by contributing to the Liberation effort. This is the 'beginning of the time' in animated communist mythology: just before the Liberation, the people resisted the Japanese, nationalists, and land owners. The stories presented in these films generate multiplying propagandistic effects by interweaving narrative motifs of anti-Japanese, anti-Kuomintang, anti-imperialist, anti-feudal, and didactic-indoctrinating storytelling. These stories do not aim at presenting an archetypal and politically required vision of one historical event but rather at designing wide visual continuum of suffering and heroism, a myriad of events that should be remembered, admired, and repeated. As a consequence, the thematical richness of the founding myth, i.e., a diversified series of events leading to Liberation, may bring out a conviction of totality and omnipresence of the doctrine which has strengthened the people's will for final victory despite the years of misery and humiliation.

Arriving at such formulated story of origin, took Shanghai animators many years of weighing and adjusting 'ingredients' of ideological and propaganda nature, and combining them with well-recognized codes of artistic communication, above all the codes of visual caricature and satire (*manhua*). In cinema's 'coming-of-age' period, Chinese animation was more frequently a subject of debates and dreams than a matter of production activities. The pioneers of animated film relied on highly limited and unprofessional production means and resources. As the film historians estimate, the whole animated production in 1931–1946 (i.e., until when the communist army overtook post-Manchukuo film studio in Changchun) counted approximately twenty titles (see Lent and Xu, *Comics Art in China* 155–156).

The historically noted production shortages should not be equaled with the lack of reflection of the future Shanghai studio's cadres on the issue of ideological function of art. Many of SAFS workers would meet before the 1949 Liberation at the Shanghai-based editorial offices of *manhua* magazines, enlisted to military troops of visual artists, or gathered in Yan'an where the revolutionary literature, graphic arts, and theater thrived, eventually they would start working at the Northeast Film Studio in Changchun. From its very beginning the animated film borrowed symbols and communicative codes from such sources as press illustrations, poster graphic art, literature, performative arts, and cinema. Changes within storytelling patterns and representation strategies observable in animated film history correspond with transformations occurring within the paradigms organizing graphic arts, a model field of artistic creativity for the pioneering animators.

From the 1910s until the 1940s, two consecutive generations of politically engaged and left-oriented artists immortalized stories about the anti-imperialist, anti-Japanese, and anti-Kuomintang resistance with the means of various forms of visual expression.

The first generation entered the scene along with the New Culture Movement, they gathered around such visionary personalities as Shen Bochen,[26] Ye Qianyu,[27] Zhang Guangyu,[28] Zhang Leping,[29] and the leading figure of Feng Zikai.[30] Commissioned by various magazines (mainly from Shanghai but also located in Guangzhou and Hong Kong), they were above all associated with *Modern Sketch* (*Shidai manhua*) published in 1934–1937. John A. Crespi summarizes this magazine's thematic and aesthetic diversity while interpreting a cut-out photo collage *The Typical Chinese Person*:[31]

> Imperialism, censorship, war, Chinese heritage, Western imports, industrialization, money-worship … all are pictured here in an absurd but arresting assemblage, one that challenges the viewer to separate calamity from humor, indignation from amusement, and the trauma of victimization from the pleasures of clever invention.
>
> (*CHINA'S MODERN SKETCH* 84)

The artists born at the early times of the New Culture Movement, who debuted as teenagers or young students, belonged to the second generation, among them Te Wei[32] and Hua Junwu.[33] In 1938, Jack Chen Yifan characterized this cohort of graphic artists:

> They do not as a group belong to any particular political party, but represent the interests of young nationally conscious intelligentsia, and they are typical of China's revolutionary students. (…) They are all former or part-time students, newspaper men, teachers, commercial artists, clerks. There are surprisingly few with a natural inclination for purely salacious humor; and ninety-nine per cent are animated by a sincere desire to save their country from colonial subjugation. This I stress, because the general level of political and national consciousness of

> Chinese artists is low. And it is a fact that there is not one avowedly reactionary cartoonist. *En masse* they are anti-imperialist, anti-feudalist. They sympathies are all with the underdog.
>
> (308 QTD. IN LENT AND XU, *COMICS ART IN CHINA* 39)

Later on, Te Wei, Zhang Guangyu, and Zhang Leping became prominent artists within SAFS structures and their artistic approaches and world views have decisively influenced the development of the Chinese animation.

These artists issued many calls for the national awakening in the light of exploitative policies of the imperialist powers as well as they directly agitated for militant actions against the Japanese occupants or corrupted Kuomintang's apparatchiks. Increasingly radicalizing, the graphic artists have established a complex network of imageries and narrations that would ideologically stimulate mass receivers. High quality artworks were released as illustrations in printed press, posters, and *lianhuanhua*, the latter being specifically structured palm-size books greatly popular with the poorer and frequently illiterate (or partially literate) social strata. Reinterpreting traditional storytelling patterns or creating original ones, these artists were dedicated to visualize the experiences of modernization and industrialization shock, charms, and drama of the urban life. The longer the occupation and Civil War lasted, the more prompted they were to thematize political issues, war ordeal, and calls for resistance. *Manhua*, a predecessor of the animation filmmaking, has anticipated the imperatives diagnosed by Tang Xiaobing in regard to the later socialist visual culture:

> the production of such a visual culture was coordinated by the new socialist state and predicated on two imperatives: to create an inspirational visual environment in

> support of the socialist revolution, on the one hand, and to invent fresh national forms by modernizing indigenous traditions and nativizing modern imports, on the other.
>
> (11)

The war film gerne, in its animated or live-action form, was meant to consolidate the nation around the conviction that the moment when the communist party overtook the power halted thousand-year-old oppression. In other words, to generate a vision of history wherein the neo-Confucian order, disintegration of the Republic ideals, and the wartime trauma would blend into 'continuum of evil' restrained only by the Liberation of the 1949. Imageries which maintained this vision consisted of image-ideas: suffering of the most vulnerable (seniors, women, children), awakening of the class consciousness and solidarity among the peasantry and workers, soldiers' readiness to sacrifice life, masses euphorically reacting to the emergence of the red flag on the horizon, etc. An impact of such image-ideas is correlated with the depictions inciting reverse emotions: grotesque characters of the traitors or brutality of the invaders. Relying on the achievements of the Shanghai critical and socially engaged art of the 1930s, the artists-ideologists of the Maoist era have gradually moved the borders between realism and uncanny hyper-realism; by synthesizing revolutionary realism and revolutionary romanticism, they have been fostering a new paradigm of a model realism. Simple motifs of the propaganda rhetoric – e.g., saturating an image with a red hue, or monumental portrayals of the mass heroes – served as dynamic and building elements of the scenes loaded with sensuality (brining out impressions of vigorousness and superagency) as well as of those which conveyed violence (fighting, struggle sessions, radical slogans).

Artistic communication operating with such semantic structures was omnipresent in the public spaces of the PRC's cities and villages during the Maoist era. Propaganda posters or popular New Year's woodcuts (*nianhua*) regularly functioned as a part of a domestic *decorum*. During the Cultural Revolution period, the inhabitants of such visual environment swiftly internalized the call for 'continuous revolution' as a summon for intensified, ideological radicalization to be performed in every sphere of life. The masses equipped with the *Red Book* descended from the propaganda posters, revolutionary *lianhuanhua* illustrations, and paintings which commemorated nameless, people's heroes of the struggle against greedy lords, corrupted Kuomintang's officials, and Japanese invaders. The myth of Liberation is a threefold equation which unifies fight for the national cause against the Japanese army, political fight with the Kuomintang, and the class struggle against the capital owners. It is a significant cultural construction, but naturally, it is one of many in a mythologized image-idea myriad construing visual environment of the Chinese communist revolution.

Animation filmmakers borrowed the structures of an 'inspiring visual environment' directly from the two generations of socially and politically engaged graphic artists. Shanghai traditions of *manhua* had to be nevertheless remolded in the spirit of the dominant doctrine. In a system which relies on integrity of a ruling party and a state as an entity (party-state system), all actions of a culture-building character solidify social conviction regarding full legitimization of the dominant system; modernization and professionalization of the culture production may, to some extent, appear as side effects of the ideological operations. The following chapters present analyses of four films made in 1947–1973 unveiling means and methods of adjusting a heritage of visual arts of the militant, anti-Japanese, and anti-Kuomintang resistance period to the rhetoric and agenda of the doctrine which prevailed after 1949.

NOTES

1. The 2012 comprehensive *Independent China* retrospective curated by Gerben Schermen presented at the Holland Animation Film Festival was a breakthrough moment for the phenomenon to

become widely recognized on the international scene of art-house animation. Among various sources discussing this specific and ambiguous phenomenon see Zhou, 2020.

2. Jan Lenica suggestively spoke about subversive potential of animated films produced in socialist Poland: "My approach towards poster and animation is similar: I have always considered both genres as means of artistic contraband. To me, poster was like a Troian horse romping across the streets and smuggling something what you do not find there normally. Animated film with its mental infantilism and visual primitivism revealed itself as a new Trojan horse capable to wrap different contents" (48). If not noted otherwise, quotations from Polish language translated by the author.
3. "Can a Communist, who is an internationalist, at the same time be a patriot? We hold that he not only can be but must be. The specific content of patriotism is determined by historical conditions. There is the 'patriotism' of the Japanese aggressors and of Hitler, and there is our patriotism. (…) For only by fighting in defence of the motherland can we defeat the aggressors and achieve national liberation. And only by achieving national liberation will it be possible for the proletariat and other working people to achieve their own emancipation. The victory of China and the defeat of the invading imperialists will help the people of other countries" (Mao, *The Role of the Chinese Communist Party*, 196).
4. "At no time and in no circumstances should a Communist place his personal interests first; he should subordinate them to the interests of the nation and of the masses" (Mao, *The Role of the Chinese Communist Party*, 198).
5. Four Wan brothers (the twins Laiming and Guchan and younger brothers, Chaochen and Dihuan) were born in Nanjing but their pursued creative career in a cosmopolitan Shanghai. 1960s' *Havoc in Heaven*, an adaptation of the classic novel *The Journey to the West* (*Xiyou ji*), is Wan Laiming's life-time achievement.
6. E.g., in *The Burning of Red Lantern Temple* (1928, dir. Zhang Shichuan). They also created a short cartoon used as a meta-filmic device in Yuan Muzhi's *City Scenes* (1935).
7. Republic of China (*Zhonghua Minguo*) was proclaimed on January 1, 1912, after the fall of the Qing Dynasty and the 1911 Xinhai Revolution, Sun Yat-sen became the first president of the new republic.

8. Marxist definitions of socio-political identity were one of many propositions discussed at that time, predominantly in the paradigms of nationalism and culturalism; the palette of views involved also are cosmopolitism, anarchism, individualism, constitutionalism, etc. See Townsend, 1992; Myers, 2000; Callahan, 2004; Xu, 2009; Pawłowski, 2013; Schneider, 2017.
9. Commenced by Beijing's students on May 4, 1919, an all-nation movement of nationalistic, anti-imperialist, anti-feudal character triggered a chain of breakthrough events in the political, social, and cultural history of China. See Teng and Fairbank, 1979; *The Appropriation of Cultural Capital*, 2001; Mitter, 2004; Gao, 2018.
10. A widespread movement of patriotic and militant character formed in 1937. The movement relied on cooperation between political units of KMT and CPC, their armed forces as well as of individual activists affiliated with different groups and other supporting associations.
11. Tang does not study animation but his argumentation is inspirational.
12. "The life of the people is always a mine of the raw materials for literature and art, materials in their natural form, materials that are crude, but most vital, rich and fundamental; (…) Some may ask, is there not another source in books, in the literature and art of ancient times and of foreign countries? In fact, the literary and artistic works of the past are not a source but a stream; (…) We must take over all the fine things in our literary and artistic heritage, critically assimilate whatever is beneficial, and use them as examples when we create works out of the literary and artistic raw materials in the life of the people of our own time and place" (Mao, *Yenan Forum*, 81).
13. See Hung, 1994; McGrath, 2010; Crespi, 2011; Pickowicz, 2012, Wang, 2017; Caschera, 2018.
14. The most notable work of Chinese-language source literature is Zhang, 2002. Du presents a list of historical and contemporary magazines dedicated to animated film (191–192). Xue Yanping discusses history of Chinese stop motion (2014). Life and work of Wan Laiming and the beginnings of SAFS are discussed in Li, 2016.
15. *Havoc in Heaven*; *Princess Peacock* (*Kong que gongzhu*, 1965, dir. Jin Xi); *Nezha Conquers Dragon King* (*Nezha nao hai*, 1979, dir. Wang Shuchen, Yan Dingxian, A Da).

16. Already Lent and Xu (2017) used this method successfully, but it is Daisy Yan Du who demonstrated extensive applicability of the interviews. She designed several projects aiming at scholarly review and edition of such sources, see *Chinese Animation and Socialism*, 2022; conference: *Animators' Roundtable Forum: Chinese Animation and (Post)Socialism*, 2017.
17. Arguably this phenomenon is correlated with the fact that the end of the Cold War and following rapid advancements in technologies of production and distribution of the film facilitated wider recognition of the contemporary Chinese cinema. This reductionist perception of Chinese cinema was to a large extent generated by critics and others outside of China, see Clark, 2021.
18. Intertwining animated film history with histories of politics, idea, and culture appears as a domain of Central-East European researchers, e.g., Midhat Ajanović (Bosnia and Herzegovina/Sweden), Michał Bobrowski, Marcin Giżycki, Hanna Margolis, Paweł Sitkiewicz (Poland), Mikhail Gurevich (Russia/USA), Anna Ida Orosz (Hungary), Ülo Pikkov (Estonia), Andrijana Ružić (Serbia/Italy).
19. Among the most famous *minzu* animations one finds, e.g., *Magic Brush* (1955, *Shenbi*, dir. Jin Xi), *Where Is Mama?* (1960, *Xiao kedou zhao mama*, dir. Te Wei, Qian Jiajun, Tang Cheng), *Havoc in Heaven*, *Cowherd and his Flute* (1963, *Mudi*, dir. Te Wei, Qian Jiajun), *Red Army Bridge* (1964, *Hongjun qiao*, dir Qian Yunda), *Nezha Conquers the Dragon King*, *Monkeys Fishing for the Moon* (1981, *Houzi lao yue*, dir. Zhou Keqin), *The Strawman* (1985, *Cao ren*, dir. Hu Jinqing), *Feelings from Mountains and Water* (1988, *Shanshui qing*, dir. Te Wei, Yan Shanchun, Ma Kexuan).
20. See Bendazzi, 2016; Quiquemelle 5; Ehrlich and Jin 10–13; Lent and Xu, *Chinese Animation Film* 116.
21. E.g., *Uproar in Heaven* (2012, *Danao tiangong*, dir. Su Da, Chen Zhihong), *Monkey King: Hero Is Back* (2015, *Xiyou ji zhi da sheng guilai*, dir. Tian Xiaopeng), *Big Fish and Begonia* (2016, *Dayu haitang*, dir. Liang Xuan, Zhang Chun).
22. For a detailed discussion see Macdonald, 2016; Lent and Xu, 2017; Du, 2019.
23. An opinion-making outlet firstly published in Shanghai, later on in Beijing, which played a pivotal role in initiating the New Culture Movement (*Xin wenhua yundong*) as well as in formulating postulates for the modern culture and society. The Kuomintang's government shut down the magazine in 1926.

24. As Tang Xiaobing writes: "In retrospect, the creation of a socialist visual culture was a grand, exhilarating project that in the mid-twentieth century, enthralled generations of Chinese artists and left behind a rich and distinct heritage. As we move farther away from the heady days of the socialist revolution, it becomes increasingly evident that the creative project of the bygone era answered forcefully the imperative of cultural transformation that was at the core of China's search for modernity. It is also clear that the project pointed to a specific vision of becoming modern" (19).
25. See Garavente, 1965; Kampen, 2000; Litten, 2001; Chang and Halliday, 2006; Li, 2007; Sun Shuyun, 2005.
26. About Shen Bochen see chapter 1.2.3 *Transcultural Perspective on Chinese Animation's Roots*.
27. Ye Qianyu created one of the most popular characters of the pre-war comics, Mr. Wang, a typical Shanghainese, pseudo-intellectual from a lower middle class whose adventures would present distorting reflection of the daily problems of Shanghai metropolis (published in 1928–1947 in *Shanghai Sketch*). During the war, Ye was a member of the National Salvation Movement. In 1949 he became a member in the presidium of the newly forming literary and arts workers organization. He fell victim to brutal, public repressions during the Cultural Revolution.
28. Zhang Guangyu was an outstanding graphic artist, illustrator, and an opinion-making commentator of the social and political life. Zhang's modernized, *manhua* adaptation *Cartoon Journey to the West* (*Xiyou manji*) was an important aesthetic reference for the production of *Havoc in Heaven*. Zhang Guangyu worked at this production as art director. It is worth adding that his brother, Zhang Zhengyu, authored background design used in the film. See Crespi, 2015; Li, 2015.
29. About Zhang Leping see chapter 1.2.4 *Visual Language of the National Salvation Movement*.
30. John Lent and Xu Ying write: "Earlier still, in the 1920s, Feng Zikai (…) exemplified 'creative adaptation', mixing contemporary social settings, humor, and religious (Buddhist) messages with Chinese brush painting and poetry, and what he had been exposed to while studying for ten months in 1921 at a school of Western painting in Japan" (*Comics Art in China* 42). The style and themes of Feng Zikai's works became politicized due to high emotional reactions he has experienced at the dawn of the Japanese invasion. The

famous work *Bombing* (*Hongzha*, 1937) presents a silhouette of a woman holding a baby, the figure is headless – instead a living fire burns on top of her neck, in the top-left corner we see an impending bomb. In the Maoist period, Feng Zikai withdrew from artistic work. See Harbsmeier, 1984; Hung 1994.

31. Unknown artist; published in Modern Sketch (*Shidai manhua*) in 1937.
32. Leader and artistic director of the SAFS from its establishment in Changchun until 1984.
33. Hua Junwu was one of the first graphic artists to reach Yan'an bases. Criticism over Hua and Ye Qianyu (from mid-1965 until January 1966) commenced the Cultural Revolution in the community of visual artists.

REFERENCES

A Companion to Chinese Cinema, edited by Zhang Yingjin, John Wiley. Blackwell Publishing, 2012.

Ai, Qing. "Tan Zhongguohua." ["On Chinese Painting."] *Wenyibao*, vol. 92, no. 15, 1953, pp. 7–9, qtd. in: Andrews 1994.

Andrews, Julia F. *Painters and Politics in the People's Republic of China, 1949–1979*. University of California Press, 1994.

Art, Politics and Commerce in Chinese Cinema, edited by Ying Zhu, Stanley Rosen, Hong Kong University Press, 2010.

Bendazzi, Giannalberto. *Animation: A World History. 1–3*. CRC Press, 2016. [Chapters, vol. 1, pp. 187-188, vol. 2, pp. 385–386, vol. 3, pp. 270–272].

Berry, Chris. *Postsocialist Cinema in Post-Mao China. The Cultural Revolution after the Cultural Revolution*, Routledge, 2004.

Burch, Noël. *To the Distant Observer. Form and Meaning in the Japanese Cinema*, revised and edited by Annette Michelson, University of California Press, 1979.

Callahan, William A. "National Insecurities: Humiliation, Salvation, and Chinese Nationalism." *Alternatives*, vol. 29, no. 29, 2004, pp. 199–218.

Caschera, Martina, "Chinese Modern Cartoon. A transcultural approach to Modern Sketch." *Altre Modernità*, vol. 2, no. 2, 2018, pp. 85–103.

Chang, Jung, Jon Halliday. *Mao: The Unknown Story*, Anchor, 2006.

Chen, Jack Yifan. "China's Militant Cartoons." *Asia*, 1938 (May), p. 308, qtd. in Lent and Xu, 2017.

Chinese Animation and Socialism: From Animators' Perspectives, edited by Daisy Yan Du, Brill, 2022.

Chomsky, Noam, Edward S. Herman. *Manufacturing Consent. The Political Economy of the Mass Media*, Bodley Head Random House, 2008.

Clark, Paul. "Generating History: Rethinking Generations in Chinese Filmmaking." *Journal of Chinese Film Studies*, vol. 1, no. 1, 2021, pp. 5–18.

Comolli, Jean-Louis, Jean Narboni. "Cinema/Ideology/Criticism." *Cahiers du Cinéma. Volume 3 1969-1972. The Politics of Representation. An anthology from "Cahiers du Cinéma" nos 210-239, March 1969-June 1972*, edited by Nick Browne, Routledge, 1996, pp. 58–67.

Crespi, John A. "Beyond Satire: The Pictorial Imagination of Zhang Guangyu's 1945 Journey to the West in Cartoons." *The Oxford Handbook of Modern Chinese Literatures*, edited by Carlos Rojas, Andrea Bachner, pp. 215–240.

Crespi, John A. *China's Modern Sketch–1, The Golden Era of Cartoon Art, 1934–1937.* MIT Visualizing Cultures, 2011. http://www.visualizingcultures.mit.edu/modern_sketch/ms_essay01.html. Accessed: 15 Dec. 2021.

Du, Daisy Yan. *Animated Encounters: Transnational Movements of Chinese Animation, 1940s-1970s*. University of Hawaii Press, 2019.

Edera, Bruno. "Animated Film in the People's Republic of China." *Animafilm*, 1980, vol. 2, no. 2, (April-June), pp. 35–41.

Ehrlich, David, Jin Tianyi. "Animation in China." *Animation in Asia and the Pacific*, edited by John A. Lent, Indiana University Press, John Libbey Publishing, 2001, pp. 7–32.

Ellul, Jacques. *Propaganda. The Formation of Men's Attitudes*. Translated by Konrad Kellen, Jean Lerner, Vintage Books Random House, 1973[1965].

Epstein, Mikhail. *After the Future: The Paradoxes of Postmodernism and Contemporary Russian Culture*, translated by Anesa Mille Pogacar, University of Massachusetts Press, 1995.

Fairbank, John King, Merle Goldman. *China. A New History*. The Belknap Press of Harvard University Press, 2006.

Farqhuar, Mary, Christopher Berry. "Shadow Opera: Toward a New Archaeology of The Chinese Cinema." *Chinese-Language Film. Historiography, Poetics, Politics*, edited by Sheldon H. Lu, Emily Yueh-yu Yeh, University of Hawaii Press, 2005, pp. 27–51.

Ferro, Marc. *Cinema and History*, translated by Naomi Greene, Wayne State University Press, 1988(1977).

Gao, Yu. *The Birth of Twentieth-Century Chinese Literature: Revolutions in Language, History and Culture*, translated by Guicang Li, Palgrave Macmillan, 2018.

Garavente, Anthony. "The Long March." *The China Quarterly*, no. 22, 1965, pp. 89–124.

Giesen, Rolf. *Chinese Animation. A History and Filmography 1922–2012*. McFarland&Company, 2015.

Góralczyk, Bogdan. *Wielki renesans. Chińska transformacja i jej konsekwencje. [Great Renaissance. Chinese Transformation and Its Consequences.]* Wydawnictwo Akademickie DIALOG, 2019.

Greenblatt, Stephen. "Towards a Poetics of Culture." *Southern Review*, vol. 20, no. 1 (March), 1987, pp. 3–15.

Harbsmeier, Christoph. *The Cartoonist Feng Zikai*. Universitetsforlaget, 1984.

Hemelryk Donald, Stephanie and Paola Voci. "China: Cinema, Politics and Scholarship." *The SAGE Handbook of Film Studies*, edited by James Donald, Michael Renov, SAGE, 2008.

Hung, Chang-tai. *War and Popular Culture. Resistance in Modern China, 1937–1945*. University of California Press, 1994.

Kampen, Thomas. *Mao Zedong, Zhou Enlai and the Evolution of the Chinese Communist Leadership*. Nordic Institute of Asian Studies, 2000.

Kołakowski, Leszek. *The Presence of Myth*, translated by Adam Czerniawski, The University of Chicago Press, 1989.

LaCapra, Dominick. *History in Transit: Experience, Identity, Critical Theory*. Cornell University Press, 2004.

Landsberger, Stefan. "The Deification of Mao: Religious Imagery and Practices During the Cultural Revolution and Beyond." *China's Great Proletarian Cultural Revolution: Master Narratives and Post-Mao Counternarratives*, edited by Woei Lien Chong, Rowman & Littlefield Publishers, 2002, pp. 139–184.

Lebel, Jean-Patrick. *Cinéma et idéologie*. Editions Sociales, 1971.

Lenica, Jan. "Jan Lenica rozmawia z redakcją Projektu. [Jan Lenica In Coversation with Project Editors.]" *Projekt*, vol. 75, no. 2, 1977, p. 48.

Lent, John A., Xu Ying. "Chinese Animation Film: From Experimentation to Digitalization." *Art, Politics, and Commerce in Chinese Cinema*, edited by Ying Zhu, Stanley Rosen, Hong Kong University Press, 2010, pp. 111–126.

Lent, John A., Xu Ying. *Comics Art in China*. University Press of Mississippi, 2017.

Leyda, Jay. *Dianying: Electric Shadows. An Account of Films and the Film Audience in China*. MIT Press, 1972.

Li, Baochuan. *Wan Laiming Yanjiu. [Study on Wan Laiming.]* Sichuan meishu chubanshe, 2016.

Li, Xiaobing. *A History of the Modern Chinese Army*. The University Press of Kentucky, 2007.

Li, Yi. *Donghua "Danao tiangong" juese biaoyan yu zaoxing zhongde 'minzuhua' guocheng. [On Cultural Nationalism analysis of Character Performance and Design in the Animation Havoc in Heaven]*. 2015. China Academy of Art. in Hangzhou, PhD dissertation.

Litten, Frederick S. "The Myth of the 'Turning Point': Towards a New Understanding of the Long March." *Bochumer Jahrbuch zur Ostasienforschung*, vol. 25, 2001, pp. 3–44.

Macdonald, Sean. *Animation in China: History, Aesthetics, Media*. Routledge, 2016.

Mao, Zedong. "On Contradiction (August 1937)." *Selected Works of Mao Tse-tung, vol. II*, Foreign Languages Press, 1965, pp. 311–345.

Mao, Zedong. "Talks at Yenan Forum on Literature and Art (May 1942)." *Quotations from Chairman Mao Tse-Tung. Selected Works, vol. III*, Foreign Languages Press, 1965, pp. 69–98.

Mao, Zedong. "The Role of the Chinese Communist Party in the National War (October 1938)." *Selected Works of Mao Tse-tung, vol. II*, Foreign Languages Press, 1965, pp. 195–212.

Marchetti, Gina. "Two Stage Sisters: The Blossoming of a Revolutionary Aesthetic." *Transnational Chinese Cinemas. Identity, Nationhood, Gender*, edited by Sheldon Hsiao-peng Lu, University of Hawaii Press, 1997, pp. 59–80.

McGrath, Jason. "Cultural Revolution Model Opera Films and the Realist Tradition in Chinese Cinema." *The Opera Quarterly*, vol. 26, no. 2–3, 2010, pp. 343–376.

Mitter, Rana. *A Bitter Revolution: China's Struggle with the Modern World*. Oxford University Press, 2004.

Myers, Ramon H. "The Chinese State during the Republican Era." *The Modern Chinese State*, edited by David Shambaugh, 2000, pp. 42–72.

Pawłowski, Józef. *Przeszłość w ideologii Komunistycznej Partii Chin. Wpływ tradycyjnej filozofii chińskiej na ideologię partii. [The Past in the Ideology of the Communist Party of China. The Impact of the Traditional Chinese Philosophy on the Party's Ideology.]* Warsaw University Press, 2013.

Perry, Elizabeth J. *Anyuan: Mining China's Revolutionary Tradition.* University of California Press, 2012.

Pickowicz, Paul G. *China on Film: A Century of Exploration, Confrontation, and Controversy.* Rowman & Littlefield Publishers, 2012.

Quiquemelle, Marie-Claire. "The Wan Brothers and Sixty Years of Animated Film in China." *Chinese Cinemas,* edited by Chris Berry, British Film Institute, 1991, pp. 175–186.

Rea, Christopher. *Animation and the Republican Chinese Film Industry.* [Association for Chinese Animation Studies], 2021, www.acas.world/2021/10/01/animation-and-the-republican-chinese-film-industry/. Accessed: 4 Jan 2022.

Schneider, Julia. *Nation and Ethnicity: Chinese Discourses on History, Historiography, and Nationalism (1900s-1920s).* Brill, 2017.

Schurmann, Franz. *Ideology and Organization in Communist China.* University of California Press, 1968.

Schwarcz, Vera. *The Chinese Enlightenment: Intellectuals and the Legacy of the May Fourth Movement of 1919.* University of California Press, 1986.

Shen, Vivien. *The Origins of Left-wing Cinema in China. 1923–37.* Routledge, 2005.

Sun, Shuyun. *The Long March.* Harper Perennial, 2006.

Sun, Xun. *Jingbang shixi gongheguo. [Republic of Jing Bang.]* Holland Animation Film Festival, 2015.

Tang, Xiaobing. *Visual Culture in Contemporary China. Paradigms and Shifts.* Cambridge University Press, 2015.

Teng, Ssu-yü, John King Fairbank. *China's Response to the West: A Documentary Survey, 1839–1923.* Harvard University Press, 1979.

Teo, Stephen. "The Opera Film in Chinese Cinema: Cultural Nationalism and Cinematic Form." *The Oxford Handbook of Chinese Cinemas,* edited by Carlos Rojas, Eileen Cheng-Yin Chow, Oxford University Press, 2013, pp. 209–224.

Teo, Stephen. *Chinese Martial Arts Cinema. The Wuxia Tradition.* Edinburgh University Press, 2009.

Terrill, Ross. *Mao: A Biography.* Stanford University Press, 1999.

The Appropriation of Cultural Capital: China's May Fourth Project, edited by Milena Dolezelova-Velingerova, Oldrich Kral, Graham Sanders, Harvard University Asia Center, 2001.

Townsend, James. "Chinese Nationalism." *The Australian Journal of Chinese Affairs,* vol. 27 (January), 1992, pp. 97–130.

Wain, Peter. *"Mao Zedong and Art." Catalogue of Mao and the Arts of New China Exhibition and Sale of Literature, Ceramics, Stone & Wood Carvings, Posters & Prints, including the Collection of Peter and Susan Wain.* Bloomsbury Auctions, 2009, pp. 4–7.

Wan, Laiming, Guchan Wan. *Wo yu Sun Wukong.* Beiyue wenyi, 1986, qtd. in Macdonald 17.

Wang, Zheng. *Finding Women in the State. A Socialist Feminist Revolution in the People's Republic of China 1949–1964.* University of California Press, 2017.

Wu, Weihua, "In Memory of Meishu Film: Catachresis and Metaphor in Theorizing Chinese Animation." *Animation Interdisciplinary Journal* (Sage), vol. 4, no. 1, 2009, pp. 32–52.

Xue, Yanping, *Zhongguo dingge donghua. [Chinese Stop Motion.].* Communication University of China Press, 2014.

Xu, Jilin. "Historical Memories of May Fourth: Patriotism, but of What Kind?" translated by Duncan Campbell, *China Heritage Quarterly,* vol. 17, 2009. China Heritage Project, The Australian National University, chinaheritagequarterly.org/features.php?searchterm=017_mayfourthmemories.inc&issue=017. Accessed: 5 May 2022.

Zhang, Huilin. *Ershi zhongguo donghua yishushi. [History of Chinese Animation in the Twentieth Century.]* Shanxi renmin chubanshe, 2002.

Zhou, Wenhai (Aaron). *Chinese Independent Animation: Renegotiating Identity in Modern China.* Palgrave Macmillan, 2020.

I

Echoes of the National Salvation Movement, 1940s–1950s

CHAPTER 1.1

Denouncing Chiang Kai-shek

The Emperor's Dream by Chen Bo'er

ORIGINATING FROM THE 1920S homemade experiments of the Wan brothers, and maturing throughout the war-torn decade of the 1930s, Chinese animated film appeared to be predisposed to intersect aesthetically and intellectually with other emerging discourses of socio-political rebellion. While the owners of film studios and cinemas (frequently operating on foreign capital) perceived animation as a supporting device limited to the quality of attraction, cohorts of *manhua* artists – graphic designers, illustrators, and cartoonists,[1] began exploring this new medium as a channel of direct, sharp, and alarmistic communication with mass audiences. As the Japanese invasion of Manchuria (1931) escalated to a state of a full-scale war (1937), national radicalism intensified among *manhua* artists, leading many of them

DOI: 10.1201/9781003241607-3

to join the ranks of revolutionary forces within the so-called National Salvation Movement. The most radical fighters soon joined the CPC (Communist Party of China) military troops in Yan'an and began preparations to overtake structures of cultural production. The future decision makers of China's cinema system were well aware of animation's mythopoeic potency, and they were determined to use it as leverage in educating and indoctrinating the young masses in line with the new, dominant doctrine. A simplistic view of Maoism identifies this doctrine as a fixed and monolithic idea of petrified codes and slogans. However, the cultural production of the Maoist period, exemplified here by animated films, demonstrates the doctrine's inner fluctuations. An ideology-oriented reading of the films may reveal the manner in which the animation medium became an expressive conglomerate of surprising visuality and engaging narrative patterns, always ready to be recycled and expanded in accordance with the new requirements of the dominant ideology.

1.1.1 UNLIKELY PIONEERS

A certain paradox is inscribed in the production history of the first Chinese puppet animation and the first socialist animated production in China, *The Emperor's Dream* (dir. Chen Bo'er, 1947).[2] Written and directed by Chen Bo'er, and animated by Mochinaga Tadahito, the film reveals the ideological premises of early People's Republic of China (PRC) cultural production. The process of formation of the Maoist cinema system began in the midst of the Civil War (1945–1949). Its structures tended to reproduce the organizing mechanisms of the Communist Party; among other patterns, it replicated the patriarchal tendency to confer spaces of decision making and advancement on the male comrades. The vision of the world expressed in the propaganda discourse of the CPC was marked by the trauma experienced under the Japanese occupation, and at the same time, it revealed the pathos and euphoria of defeating the Axis powers in World War II. The discourse itself was determined by the methods of agitation operating in two significant realms of persuasion: the political struggle against American influences, and the social struggle addressed to the urban and countryside inhabitants who had grown tired of Kuomintang (KMT, Chinese Nationalist Party) governance. Such premises intensified the nationalistic features of the new symbolic order; nevertheless, the initial strategies of Chinese animated film development were designed by two unusual figures for such a patriarchal power structure: the female director Chen Bo'er and the Japanese master of puppet film Mochinaga Tadahito.[3]

Chen Bo'er, a star of the Shanghai silver screens, became interested in communist ideology and avant-garde theater in the end of the 1920s. In the 1930s and the 1940s, she frequently contributed various journalistic reports, as well as articles on the theory of culture, to feminist magazines. She worked as an actress, director, and cultural activist in Shanghai and Hong Kong, to where she had fled due to political persecution of the group she was affiliated with. In 1938, Chen reached a communist base in Yan'an where she organized revolutionary performances. In 1946, she joined the Northeast Film Studio in Changchun as a director and producer. From 1949 until her premature death in 1951, she was directly involved in the establishment of the New China cinema studio system and the foundation of the Performing Arts Institution (later renamed the Beijing Film Academy).

Mochinaga Tadahito grew up in Manchuria and graduated from the Academy of Fine Arts in Tokyo. His first animations made in Japan propagated Emperor Hirohito's policies.[4] In early 1945, he was hired by the art department of the Man-El (Manchukuo Film Association) film studio controlled by the Imperial Army. When the Japanese forces began evacuation, he stayed in Manchuria voluntarily and began teaching animation art and craft to Chinese revolutionary artists aspiring to become animators. Mochinaga left the PRC in 1953, seen off with deep regret by his students-friends, some of whom already held prominent positions at the film studio in Shanghai. They met again only in 1988 when the first Chinese international animated film festival in Shanghai rolled out the red carpet for its guests. Mochinaga's work is a frequently studied subject in Asian animation and commercial industry studies (see Ono, 1999; Clements, 2013; Du, 2019), and the artist's grand-daughter Mochinaga Noriko actively popularizes his heritage on the festival and gallery circuit. Taking a closer look at Chen Bo'er as a theoretician, film director, and film culture activist may broaden the understanding of the intellectual and ideological background of the founders of Chinese animation.[5]

Chen's revolutionary spirit manifested itself for the first time in 1911 when the five-year-old future Party secretary of the Changchun Film Studio and director of the artistic department at the Central Film Bureau horrified the good folk of the small town of Anbu in Guangdong province by cutting off her long pigtail (see Wang 144). Her film-acting career came in the 1930s, and as an insider in the pop-culture industry, she personally experienced the consequences of adopting a Westernized, patriarchal model of show business. In 1936, the magazine *Women's Life (Funü shenghuo)* published her harshly insightful theoretical text *The Female-Centered Film and the Male-Centered Society*. Thirty-nine years before Laura Mulvey, Chen Bo'er discussed the problematic instance of the 'male gaze',[6] and argued the necessity of empowering women's emancipation in cultural production and popular reception. Simultaneously, Chen advocated the idea of national salvation. Alike other intellectuals involved in the communist movement (specifically those active in the field of cinema such as Xia Yan[7] and Yuan Muzhi,[8] her future husband), Chen Bo'er perceived anti-feudal struggle above all as a path to women's liberation. Furthermore, she asserted that all frontlines of the revolutionary fight (anti-feudalism, anti-imperialism, resistance to Japanese occupation, new cultural movements, etc.) jointly served the major cause, defined as a national cause. As a pioneer of Chinese feminist thought, Chen Bo'er was determined to turn her ideas into artistic practice, and to that end, deliberately chose such roles in film productions that would portray women characters as active, decisive, and conscious of the aims and methods of the revolutionary struggle.[9] Already in the Yan'an period, and particularly after 1946 when she assumed a leading position at the Changchun studio, Chen dedicated her time to organizing work (designing and implementing the operating structures of the cinema and film education system) and writing (contributing to the formulation of the aesthetic principles of New China cinema).

Among Chen's varied theoretical achievements, it is worth mentioning a production premise that was also adopted later on by filmmakers from the Shanghai Animation Film Studio:[10] *xia shenghuo* ('enter life'). According to the Maoist model of cinema, film production was a collective affair; therefore, the filmmakers had to confront their creative concepts with other artists as well as representatives of the groups portrayed in a given film. Chen argued that the paradigm of realism, and cinema's obligation to serve the people, calls for conducting preparations as a certain form of 'field research'. According to this principle, the collectives should set out into the field (searching for the most authentic locations possible), and familiarize themselves with the living conditions, the needs and ambitions of its inhabitants, achievements, and shortages determining the local social existence. This method became institutionalized in the Maoist cinema production system. Distorted over the course of time, *xia shenghuo* has eventually absorbed a form of a hollow ritual, and sometimes even a mechanism of oppression. In the beginning, however, this praxis generated opportunities for close encounters between the filmmakers (who grew artistically in lieu of the conventional realism of the 1930s) and the portrayed masses (whose representatives were discovering cinema for themselves, sometimes for the first time in their lives). In 1951 Chen Bo'er participated in the infamous campaign against the film *The Life of Wu Xun* and the persecution of its director Sun Yu. She died of a heart attack suffered after leaving a filmmakers' gathering where she called fellow comrades to criticize her.

1.1.2 HOPELESS DREAMS OF THE BYGONE ERA

The Emperor's Dream is mentioned in each study of Chinese animation; however, very rarely is the film discussed in detail.[11] Premiering on May 1, 1947, it is the tenth episode in the fourth newsreel series *Democratic Northeast* (*Minzhu dongbei di si ji (10): Huangdi meng*).[12] The film was restored by the China Film Archive, but it is shown to international audiences only on rare occasions, and even then the screening copy consists of only the first fourteen minutes of the film.[13] Regardless of these shortcomings, the excerpt provides an intriguing conceptual framework for the analysis of its ideological content. The available material can be divided into two parts. The first part stylistically maintains typical tropes of the 1940s' propaganda: ironic comments are inscribed into props present in the diegetic space, or pronounced by the omniscient voice-over narrator. The simple means of expression strongly increase the derogatory effect of propagandistic communication. Chiang Kai-shek (KMT leader) meets with General George Marshall in order to make a wicked deal: Chinese natural resources will be sold in exchange for US military support. The latter segment is set on the opera stage featuring the Generalissimo, subsequently joined by four animal characters representing conflicting factions of the KMT. This sequence breaks away from the convention of caricature, replacing it with surrealism. As the title suggests, Chiang Kai-shek dreams of having the emperor's power; however, the structure of the preserved excerpt does not manifest transitions between reality and fantasy. In other words, no expressive device was used to facilitate changes within the filmic reality (e.g., defocus transition). The world presented in the film exists only in the register of delusion, exaggeration, and grotesque, and its inhabitants have no means or ways of escape.

Despite its general straightforwardness, the first part demonstrates certain features of bizarreness and estrangement.[14] What is of more significance, from the very beginning of the film, the viewers' process of locating the diegesis suffers disorder. The first shot presents an abstract stage of a highly disturbing decorum. A swastika catches viewers' attention as an element repeatedly used in rich ornamentation, and a symbol of a hostile ideology contended by Chinese communists. Regardless of the swastika's centuries-old religious connotations in Asian cultures, its contemporary meaning related to Nazism was well known to wartime audiences, the artists of the national salvation *manhua* frequently employed the image of the swastika when emphasizing the necessity of international solidarity in the struggle against fascism.[15] A board that reads "Do not make any noise" is positioned center stage; it is revealed to the viewers in a slow zoom shot. Simultaneously a female voice-over informs the spectators that they are looking at the stage upon which Chiang Kai-shek has been performing a horrible and anti-democratic spectacle of massacre for twenty years, and he silences any voice of criticism. With the simple contrast between the blunt voice-over and the restrictive element of set design, the first strings of revolutionary emotions are moved. An accusatory speech continues to the sounds of percussion instruments. Emotional and ideological tensions surge. After the cut, the location changes to Chiang's office. Utterly different from the previous space, the crude and raw interior does not seem to be in any way connected to the highly symbolic opera stage.

General Marshall's entrance to Chiang's chambers instigates action whereby traitors and imperialists do not have the right to speak up (they cannot make any sound); instead, it is the female narrator who explains the situation and denounces the malicious intentions of the conspirators. Extra-diegetic narration is complemented with various writings that appear in the filmic reality inscribed on documents and maps. Their contents ironically reveal imperialistic and anti-patriotic meanings of the American–Kuomintang intrigue. The movement of all the wooden puppets is far from fluid, but it is the figurine of General Marshall that appears most clumsy, and a grotesque, false smile is painted on his face. The puppet of Chiang Kai-shek is strictly caricatural: ridiculously thin and short, he 'sinks' under vast, traditional clothing. His disproportionally high forehead and protruding ears vividly contrast with a comically tampered face. His characteristic mustache hangs above a clenched, almost triangular jaw. The character design was based on caricatures drawn by Hua Junwu, one of the leading graphic artists from Yan'an whose art of national salvation was very well known among the communist troops and their sympathizers. As soon as Chiang and Marshall shake hands on the deal, the Generalissimo sees himself in the mirror wearing an imperial tiara. General Marshall embraces this vision, but he reminds Chiang that there is still one more spectacle to be performed. The American official hands over the *jing*[16] mask, but the Republican president chooses to wear the mask of a 'good father of the nation': a sincere, smiling, and chubby face which differs greatly from Chiang's real visage. As the voice-over narrator comments, "[T]he real killer, American imperialism, everybody knows what they are aiming for. Chiang Kai-shek is wearing his hypocrisy mask and put on some perfume of democracy. But no matter what he does, he cannot fool our people anymore".

A display of the posters promoting Chiang Kai-shek's performances serves as a transition imagery from the sequence of negotiations to the spectacle. The affiches dating from 1927 provide information on Kuomintang crimes (the April 12 Purge,[17] the fight against the communists, the lack of resistance against the Japanese Imperial Army, and imperial court restitution attempts), and the last one credits the United States as the director of the performance. The visual design of the posters merges the swastika with the sun, the symbol of the Kuomintang, which directly equates the KMT government with the Third Reich. Eventually, the viewer looks once again at the opera stage. Only now do the two distant localities of the filmic reality become integrated. Chiang enters wearing a mask of cordiality and a hat of a serving official, his backwards walk resembles an awkward dance. Several featureless puppets sit still in the audience. Chiang puts forward a roll of documents filled with noble declarations ("People's Political Consultative Conference"; "Listen to the people"; "The Five Decisions"; "Peace treaty"). The camera, transiting from full shots to medium close-ups, keeps changing the point of view, placing the eye of the viewer in front of as well as behind the puppet. Thanks to this operation, the viewers can decipher the writings on the back of the roll, slogans of hatred for political enemies, contempt for the people, and the self-worship of the dictator.

Once the ritual of hypocrisy concludes, four servile animals appear on the stage to sit on an assembly.[18] These grotesque minions represent various factions of the right-wing political spectrum of the period.[19] A dog symbolizes the inner KMT faction Political Study Clique (*Zhengxue*), a fox connotes the China Democratic Socialist Party (*Zhongguo minzhu shehuidang*), a monkey represents the Chinese Youth Party (*Zhongguo qingnian dang*), while a pig stands for various local leaders. Chiang resides upon the assembly from the heights of an imperial throne and declares himself a dictator while the animals kneel. He announces changes in the government, and the animals immediately start to bark, yelp, squeal, and fight. This intentionally chaotic and eerie sequence generates a transgressive impression as the performed, degenerated power ritual appears to extend the limits of the viewers' comprehension. At some point, Chiang brings out a piece of raw meat. In the course of the 'meat-fight' scene, the logic of locating diegesis becomes disturbed once again. Chiang, shown in a medium shot sitting on the throne, puts the meat forward on a stick, as if he was fishing. The camera cuts sharply, and the viewers look at the meat in a close-up. The flesh is located on a homogeneous, black background, fully abstract from any reality recognized so far by the spectators. The haunch is swarmed with ants and the sounds of barking and oinking radically increase. This whole shot lasts no longer than a few seconds, but it leaves a powerful impression which on the one hand brings out a strong sensation of disgust, and on the other hand, it awakes visual associations with European avant-garde cinematic experiments. After another sharp cut, the stage appears in a wide shot, disclosing animals quarreling under the presidential stool. Suddenly a thunderstorm is heard and a lightning strike breaks up the fight. The fearful animals bow down in front of their master and disperse around the stage as if they were parodying Bruegel's parable of the blind. Here the preserved excerpt ends.

Regarding the fact that *The Emperor's Dream* is a segment in a wartime film chronicle, the question of its relationship to the historical reality *de facto* concerns its relationship with the political reality at the time of its production. Regardless of the country of origin, 20th-century wartime animated production above all served the purpose of boosting military morale. The humorous, phantasmagorical animated forms infused with indoctrinating messages were addressed to the widest possible mass audience, as in its most generalized nature, the animated film medium does not impose any prerequisites concerning viewers' age or level of education. The characters' gallery from *The Emperor's Dream* may suggest an assumption of a high level of information in regard to the current political situation among the viewers. Naturally, the general public was well familiar with Chiang Kai-shek as well as General Marshall; however, referring to the actors of the internal KMT political struggle suggests that in the course of the Civil War, wider groups of potential viewers showed deeper interest in the political transformation occurring in the country. The debacle of the negotiations between communists and nationalists led by General Marshall (January 1947), Chiang Kai-shek's tactical and strategic mistakes generating subsequent military defeats, and dramatic inflation increasing poverty and hunger in the cities as well as in the provinces ruled by KMT,[20] were all factors which fueled and radicalized the atmosphere among society which was becoming increasingly in favor of the CPC.[21] The political reality revealed in the film is of a direct and terse character when referring to complicated but publicly well-known situations. The mode of condensed symbolism serves to convey a view of historical reality as long-lasting oppression. This strategy relies on the use of metaphors of a mask and a fight. Opera decorum and Chiang's performance visualize his political *modus operandi*. Multiple theatrical affiches remind the viewers of decades marked with grief and death. The piece of rotten meat symbolizes Chiang Kai-shek's perception of China and its people.

The enemy, danger, sacrifice, and victory belong to the major and universal themes of all propaganda communication. Michał Bobrowski, analyzing the phenomenon of conjoined symmetry between American and Soviet Cold War-era animated propaganda, comments on a perverse strategy of reproducing the enemy's propaganda in order to deform and disturb its meanings (a mechanism that he traces back to the wartime filmmaking output of Frank Capra):

> The 'recycled' propagandistic images of the Axis's strength and power that were originally aimed at stimulating national pride and unity, in the new context, fulfill a new function – the function of stirring up the emotion of fear. (…) In order to use fear without damaging the troops' morale, the authors had to combine this emotion with an unshakable conviction about the moral and civilizational superiority of the 'free world' over the 'slave world'.
>
> (BOBROWSKI 51)

Even if Chen Bo'er's film 'recycles' only a minor fraction of the KMT's propaganda (slogans presented by Chiang to the opera's audience), it is fully focused on representing the world of the enemy. As such, it maintains a key dichotomy of 'us versus them' in constructing its indoctrinative meaning. The enemy's world is built from disturbing, or even disgusting, images, while the voice-over narration, its slogans and calls, discursively establish foundations of the new, positive world order. Subjective qualities (the dream metaphor, the transgression of a ritual, and the ambiguity of the spectacle) are contrasted and valuated against objective qualities of reality (the voice-over commentary 'calls things by their real name', e.g., the people are victorious, the enemies of the people are evil).

Beside the fact that Mochinaga was a well-trained puppet animator, the choice of this technique might have corresponded with the authors' intention to invoke associations with the tradition of puppet and marionette theater, an art form particularly popular in the north-eastern regions (see F. P. Chen 2017). Chiang's performance immediately conveys the metaphor of politics as theater, while the expressive means that generate estrangement and exaggeration establish the presented reality as a farcical illusion. The Kuomintang leader is a comedian who does not dare to wear a *jing* mask, which is an attribute of an opera character who – even if sometimes morally ambivalent – remains an instance driven by self-agency, described in the categories of fright, admiration, and respect. The level of grotesque of this absurd reality surges along with the appearance of the animals acolytes. The meaningful elements of costume design (such as swastikas and a human skull on Chiang's robe), sinister sound effects (howling, drumming, but also the silencing of the enemies in the first segment), and startling editing (disorder in locating diegesis as well as the shot of a piece of rotten meat): all such means and devices of expression sustain the great derision upon which *The Emperor's Dream* is based. An evident accumulation of the means of an estrangement within the film neutralizes the realistic convention typical of propaganda. Such an intentional discrepancy attests to the phenomenon of Maoist propaganda being a changeable-in-time discourse. What seems a doctrinal inconsistency from the time distance should be contextualized as an element of a diversified cultural production, solid and convergent in its particular, temporary functions.

1.1.3 'CONVENIENT TRUTHS' AT THE STAGE OF NEW DEMOCRACY

For the sake of full propagandistic clarity, the first segment is complemented with a voice-over narration. The texts uttered with the greatest emphasis express anti-American and anti-imperialist contents as well as disdain for Chiang Kai-shek's betrayal. Further on, the voice-over narration is replaced with the presentation of two-sided meanings on the rolls. The KMT leader's act of hypocrisy consists of abusing the rhetoric of democracy while his actions demonstrate the will of autocratic rule. The Maoists of the mid-1940s regarded the struggle for a 'new democracy' as a question of ideological and social integrity; its aims and methods were formulated by Mao Zedong in 1940. Mao presented the current condition of the Chinese state as a country which was partially colonized, partially semi-colonized, and as a whole oppressed by the imperialists as well as bureaucratic and military governance. At that time, the communist leader assumed that regardless of its manifold demerits and general mediocrity, the Chinese bourgeoisie could become an ally of the communist revolutionaries in the struggle against imperialistic oppressiveness. However, he remained convinced that allowing the bourgeoisie to lead the struggle would be a costly mistake[22] – expensive in the sense that it would slow down the revolution, a process that required fulfillment in two phases. The first phase relied on building the system of a 'new democracy' that would maintain the three principles of Sun Yat-sen,[23] and an alliance of all revolutionary classes. The second phase concerned the socialist revolution adopted to the social and cultural specifics of the Chinese civilization (*guoqing*). Advocating for 'new democracy', Mao directly attacked the Kuomintang as a force responsible for obstructing social progress through lies and national betrayal. The 'big lie', as Mao claimed, was to be found in the official rhetoric of the National Party embracing the power of the people, while: "[F]or sixteen years the Kuomintang has violated this declaration and as a result it has created the present grave national crisis" (Mao 352). To fight the communists, he argued, is to perform an act of national betrayal: "Opposition to communism is the policy of the Japanese imperialists (…) No matter whom you follow, the moment you oppose the Communist Party you become a traitor, because you can no longer resist Japan" (Mao 365). Such premises are explicitly enunciated in *The Emperor's Dream*; they belong to the core content of the spoken and written calls and slogans addressed to the audience in order to shape and strengthen their understanding of the film, the current fight, and the general vision of the world.

As Mao wrote in a further passage: "[A] given culture is the ideological reflection of the politics and economics of a given society" (Mao 369); thus, the state of a 'new democracy' does not exist without the established principles of a 'new culture'. Cultural issues were of high relevance to the commander of the Chinese revolution, and he dedicated much thought to this concern in the discussed text. Revolutionary culture demands "sweeping away" the reactionary one (the one that serves the needs of the imperialists and feudal lords): "There is no construction without destruction, no flowing without damming and no motion without rest; the two are locked in a life-and-death struggle" (Mao 369). An animated film, as a new medium characterized by the lack of centennial traditions and well-established conventions, was welcomed by the Changchun Film Studio creative cadres as a perfect device in the revolutionary struggle. The authors of *The Emperor's Dream*, the first socialist animated production, initiated the process of constructing the aesthetics and conventions of the new medium. In this context, it should be noted that the question regarding the relationship between new socialist art and Chinese cultural heritage immediately became as important as ambiguous concern for the film theory, aesthetics, and practice. On the one hand, Chiang Kai-shek's performance is dubbed by the voice-over narrator as a "spectacle in an old style"; as such, it evokes regressive cultural archaisms. On the other hand, one notices that the traditional performative forms function as a source of artistic inspirations – puppet theater, the requisites borrowed from the opera tradition (above all the stage and the mask), and traditional folk music heard in the sound score. What is more, these elements facilitate the emergence of a surrealist aura (a category borrowed from Western culture). The encounter (or clash) of traditional and surreal qualities appears inherently interwoven with the major ideological message of the film. The mockery of the feudal society and its collaborators (Chiang Kai-shek, General Marshall, KMT factions) simultaneously articulates the aims and methods of a revolutionary struggle (voice-over), and visualizes communist art's potency to absorb both traditional and modern artistic, intellectual, and social tendencies (the theatrical sequence).

The character of the 'new democracy' culture envisioned by Mao Zedong was revolutionary, national (detached from reactionary, imperialistic cultures), scientific (contrary to the superstitions of the feudal era), and mass (democratic). However, the 'new-democratic' cultural production was supposed to avoid the trap of an oversimplified indoctrination. Instead, the 'new culture' would pursue such artistic and intellectual modes of creativity that could entertain both the masses and their allies recruiting from the national bourgeoisie class. Eventually, the 'new art' would consciously reinterpret patterns of traditional expression, extracting regressive, feudal contents from those which solidify and testify to the uniqueness of the Chinese national and cultural identity. Such was the advised mode of approaching the inspirational foreign artistic tendencies – sweeping imperialist reaction away but not turning away from its subversive and demystifying potential. The propagandistic efficiency was the rudimentary requirement bestowed upon Chen Bo'er, Mochinaga Tadahito, and other members of the creative crew from Changchun. Informed by their intellectual and artistic biographies, historians may assume that the development of ideological consciousness and improvement of artistic creativity were perceived as intertwining and mutually conditioning spheres of reflection. As Mao himself said: "However, we must keep the spreading of communist ideas and propaganda about the communist social system distinct from the practical application of the new-democratic program of action; (…) It is undoubtedly inappropriate to mix the two up" (379–380). Here one finds the framework (and limitations) of the artistic freedom of expression in the 'new-democratic' phase. This 'convenient truth' had ceased to serve its purpose by 1949 at the dawn of the People's Republic of China.

NOTES

1. *Manhua* functions as an umbrella term for the art of cartoons and comic strips realized in diverse styles, genres, and techniques.
2. Daisy Yan Du (2019) proposes the translation of the title *Huangdi meng* as *Dreaming to Be Emperor* as more suitable to the film's storyline. Agreeing with Du, I nonetheless keep the title *The Emperor's Dream* as already widely recognized among researchers of Chinese animation.
3. The Chinese names of Mochinaga Tadahito are Fang Ming and Zhiyong Zhiren.
4. "When he graduated, Mochinaga was hired by the animation department of Geijutsu Eigasha (GES, Art Film Company), where he worked with famed World War II animator Seo Mitsue on *Ari-Chan* (*Ant-Boy*) and *Momotaro, The Sea Eagle*, an important propaganda film commissioned by the Japanese Imperial Navy in 1943" (Lent and Xu 159).
5. Chen Bo'er's name is mentioned in all English language studies that bring up *The Emperor's Dream* and her second directorial cell animation *Go After an Easy Prey* (*Wengzhongzhuobie*, 1949), but John A. Lent and Xu Ying were the first researchers to dedicate several paragraphs to her work (see Lent and Xu 161-162). Extensive analysis of Chen's acting, live-action filmmaking, and theoretical output is presented in Wang 2017.
6. Chen Bo'er appears as a pioneer in the field of feminist film theory who was distinctly ahead of her time in both the local as well as the international context of 1930s' film reflection. The following passage appears especially significant: "In a male-centered society, politics, the economy, and all the ruling powers are in men's hands. Thus all the laws, morality, customs, and norms are shaped by men's biased positions. Aesthetic views are no exception. They too are shaped by men's biased preferences … Women

in such a society have unconsciously conformed to its demands. For instance, using makeup was not originally in women's nature, but in order to cater to the preferences of a male-centered society it has become female nature. This explains why female audiences have similar views toward female stars as that of male audiences. The difference is that the male audience's view expresses the direct preference out of a dominator's psychology, while the female audience's view arises from the psychology of the dominated to unconsciously cater to the preferences of the dominator" (B. Chen 1936: 62–64, qt. in Wang 150).

7. Xia Yan, 1900–1995, playwright, scriptwriter, and cultural theorist. In 1919, he co-founded the magazine *Zhejiang Xinchao*, and his articles caught the attention of Chen Duxiu, the first leader of the CPC. In 1927, Xia translated August Babel's treatise *Die Frau und der Sozialismus* (1879) which became a fundamental work for the emerging Chinese feminist movement. Xia Yan's theatrical plays confronted social and sexual norms that were tabooed and repressed in the world regulated by the feudal, bourgeois, and colonial order. His deeply patriotic works were also aimed at the modernization of Chinese theatre conventions (the plays *Sai Jinhua*, 1936; *Qiu Jin*, 1944). In the 1930s, encouraged by members of the CPC, Xia Yan infiltrated the most powerful Chinese film studio, Mingxing, where he agitated among the filmmakers and workers for the so-called progressive cinema. He joined the CPC, spent time in Yan'an, and became a member of the artistic and literary troops within the National Salvation Movement. In 1949–1954, he supervised the consolidation of the Chinese cinema studio system structures, and in 1955–1964, he served as a deputy minister of culture responsible for cinema. The film projects he supported (frequently as a script consultant) were often subject to political criticism (e.g., *Two Stage Sisters/Wutai jiemei*, 1964, dir. Xie Jin; *Early Spring in February/Zaochun eryue*, 1964, dir. Xie Tieli), while other films turned out to be highly successful (*New Year's Sacrifice/Zhu fu*, 1956, dir. Sang Hu; *A Revolutionary Family/Geming jiating*, 1961, dir. Shui Hua). From June 1964 to April 1965, Xia Yan became a target of oppressive criticism; deprived of his functions, he spent the next eight years in prison.
8. Yuan Muzhi, 1909–1978, actor, director, and prominent member of the early PRC's cinema institutions. In 1937 together with Chen Bo'er and Xia Yan, Yuan joined the China Film Circles Wartime Resistance Association (*Zhonghua quanguo dianying jie kang di*

hui). The three artists collaborated on the highly popular, patriotic, and anti-Japanese war movie *800 Heroes* (*Babai zhanshi*, 1938, dir. Ying Yunwei). In Yan'an, Yuan Muzhi focused on directing newsreels. In 1939, he was preparing for a documentary film production. Eventually the film was not made even though Yuan left for Moscow to proceed with post-production (the footage was left behind by the staff evacuating the studio on July 22, 1941). Yuan Muzhi stayed in the USSR until November 1945, studying Soviet film theories under Sergei Eisenstein. He returned to the Northeast studio in Changchun to take a leading position, and in 1949, he was transferred to the Central Film Bureau. Xia Yan was responsible for the transformation process of the New China's studio system (the nationalization of ramified private production and distribution centers), but it was Yuan Muzhi who designed the implemented changes. He also supervised the professionalization of production conditions in collaboration with experts from Czechoslovakia. After the campaign against the film *The Life of Wu Xun*, and Chen Bo'er's death, the antagonistic pro-Soviet faction made him step down from his position.

9. Films directed by Ying Yunwei: *800 Heroes*, *Plunder of Peach and Plum* (*Taoli jie*, 1934), *Revolutionaries* (*Shengsi tongxin*, 1936), and *On Youth* (*Qingchun xian*, 1934, dir. Yao Sufeng).
10. The creative crew of the famous ink-wash animations *The Cowherd's Flute* and *Feelings from Mountains and Water* spent some time during the pre-production period studying local landscapes and customs in Guangdong Province and in the area of Fuchun River in Zhejiang Province, respectively (see Lent and Xu 166).
11. Daisy Yan Du's book *Animated Encounters* ... is an exception in this regard. The author summarizes the plot, explains production conditions at the Changchun studio, and presents the plot summary (Du 92–95).
12. Film chronicles in the series *Minzhu dongbei* were produced from mid-1949 (see Gao 2009).
13. To the author's best knowledge, her curated program *Daughters of the Revolution. Women Filmmakers in Classic Chinese Animation* presented at the Tricky Women/Tricky Realities International Animation Festival in Vienna in 2019 was the first European screening of the film. As a result of the dedicated efforts of the festival's organizers, the China Film Archive provided the excerpt for the screening. This short version was also screened during *The*

Inaugural Conference of the Association for Chinese Animation Studies, Zoom Webinar, organized by the Hong Kong University of Science and Technology in March–May 2021. The original complete film's runtime is twenty minutes (Du 92).

14. E.g., Chiang Kai-shek's headquarters is located at the opera's dressing room; the flower basket and elegant perfumes gifted by Marshall symbolize tanks and imperialist ideas. The symbolic meanings of Marshall's gifts are explained by the writings inscribed on the props.
15. E.g., Ye Qianyu's *manhua* work: *The New Lines of Battle?* published in Modern Sketch between 1934 and 1937 (see Crespi 21).
16. The so-called 'painted-face', a typical character of the Beijing opera.
17. Also known as the Shanghai Massacre, denoting the persecution of Shanghai communists ordered by Chiang Kai-shek that led to arrests which concluded in harsh sentencing, executions, and people going missing. On April 12, workers' unions clashed with law enforcement; in the course of brutal fighting, around 300 people were wounded or lost their lives, and from a long-term perspective, tens of thousands of communists in various provinces were subject to persecution. The KMT's political history addresses this event as an element of a struggle among the factions, while in the historical memory of the CPC, the April 12 Purge stands for one of the most important martyrological stories.
18. This scene may be read either as a parody of the National Assembly of November 15, 1946, that was not attended by the representatives of the CPC, or manipulated parliamentary elections of March 1947.
19. Each character's appearance is accompanied with an explanatory writing.
20. Importantly, the communist propaganda compared the tragic economic conditions experienced under the KMT government with the social optimism in regard to early attempts at land reform initiated in the regions controlled by the communists.
21. At the turn of 1945 and 1946, almost the entire army of the former Manchukuo state (counting 75,000 people) joined the People's Liberation Army (PLA). In the March 1947 parliamentary elections, the PMs representing regions engulfed in the Civil War were designated by the government; therefore, the scale of the support for Chiang Kai-shek's rule was significantly manipulated. Furthermore: "Until the end of 1947 the numbers of Kuomintang's

armies was reduced by nearly two-thirds. In most cases they joined the enemy's side. In the middle of 1948 CPC counted over 3 million people, among them 2.5 million who served in the People's Liberation Army" (Gacek 196).

22. "Possible participation in the revolution on the one hand, and proneness to conciliation with the enemies of the revolution on the other – such is the dual character of the Chinese bourgeoisie, it faces both ways (...) Therefore, the proletariat, the peasantry, the intelligentsia and the other sections of the petty bourgeoisie undoubtedly constitute the basic forces determining China's fate (...) The Chinese democratic republic which we desire to establish now must be a democratic republic under the joint dictatorship of all anti-imperialist and anti-feudal people led by the proletariat," (Mao 349–350).
23. The 'Three Principles of the People' (*sanmin zhuyi*) embrace nationalism (*minzu*), democracy (*minzhu*), and welfare rights (*minsheng*).

REFERENCES

Bobrowski, Michał. "Ideological Hall of Mirrors. Reflections of Soviet Propaganda in American Propaganda of the 1940s and 1950s." *Propaganda, Ideology, Animation, Twisted Dreams of History*, edited by Olga Bobrowska, Michał Bobrowski, Bogusław Zmudziński, AGH University of Science and Technology Press, 2019, pp. 39–68.

Chen, Bo'er. "Nüxing zhongxin de dianying yu nanxing zhongxin de shehui. [The Female-Centered Film and the Male-Centered Society.]" *Funü shenghuo* 1936, no. 2, pp. 62–64, qtd. in Wang 150.

Chen, Fan Pen, Li. *Marionette Plays from Northern China*. State University of New York Press, 2017.

Clements, Jonathan. *Anime. A History*. Bloomsbury Publishing, 2013.

Crespi, John. *China's Modern Sketch–1, The Golden Era of Cartoon Art, 1934–1937*. MIT Visualizing Cultures, 2011, www.visualizingcultures.mit.edu/modern_sketch/ms_essay01.html. Accessed: 15 Dec. 2021.

Du, Daisy, Yan. *Animated Encounters: Transnational Movements of Chinese Animation, 1940s-1970s*. University of Hawaii Press, 2019.

Gacek, Łukasz. *Chińskie elity polityczne w XX wieku [Chinese Political Elites in the Twentieth Century]*. Księgarnia Akademicka, 2008.

Gao, Weijin. *Minzhu dongbei de shezhi [Filming of Democratic Northeast]*. Zhongyang xinying jituan [Central New Film Group], 2009, www.cndfilm.com/20090604/107544.shtml. Accessed: 4 Jan 2022.

Lent, John A., Xu, Ying. *Comics Art in China*. University Press of Mississippi, 2017.

Mao, Zedong. "On New Democracy (January 1940)." *Selected Works of Mao Tse-tung, vol. II*, Foreign Languages Press, 1965, pp. 339–384.

Ono, Kosei. "Tadahito Mochinaga: The Japanese Animator Who Lived in Two Worlds." *Animation World Magazine* 4.9, Dec. 1999, www.awn.com/mag/issue4.09/4.09pages/onomochinaga3.php3. Accessed: 15 Dec. 2021.

Wang, Zheng. *Finding Women in the State. A Socialist Feminist Revolution in the People's Republic of China 1949–1964*. University of California Press, 2017.

CHAPTER 1.2

Unity in Resistance

Wanderings of Sanmao by Zhang Chaoqun

In the Northeast Film Studio in Changchun, Chen Bo'er and Mochinaga Tadahito have established structural, production, and technological foundations of the animation department which transformed in the 1950s into an autonomous institution, the Shanghai Animation Film Studio (SAFS). Several graphic designers and illustrators proved their skills in using visual communication as a means of mass mobilization during the wars with Japan and Kuomintang. This cohort was entrusted with delineating a direction of an animated film development in New China. Ideological in its nature, such decision went against a typical organizing model of international film studios which were artistically led by the well-recognized filmmakers and inventors of animated film technologies (e.g., Walt Disney or Fleischer Brothers in the United States). In the 1940s, the animated feature, *Princess Iron Fan* (*Tie shan gongzhu*, 1941, dir. Wan Laiming, Wan Guchan), was highly popular with the wide audience both domestically and

DOI: 10.1201/9781003241607-4

in the region. Despite adhering to the patriotic principles, none of the siblings-pioneers have joined military artistic brigades, and in the mid-1940s, the brothers have stayed away from the China mainland. Te Wei, an important revolutionary graphic artist, was appointed to the directorial position at the animation department. The future SAFS leader did not have any previous experience with animation;[1] since 1931, he has published patriotic, anti-Japanese, and anti-Kuomintang illustrations in the Shanghai magazines, and in autumn 1938, he became a lead officer of a partially militant, partially artistic National Salvation Cartoon Propaganda Corps (*Jiuwang manhua xuanchuandui*). Zhang Leping, the author of *Sanmao* – "the most popular strip in Chinese cartoon history" (Lent and Xu, *Comics Art in China* 25) – was a leader of the second brigade with the corps. Soon after the formation of the department, the Shanghai animators started working on an adaptation of this famous comic, and Zhang Leping collaborated with them as a co-author of a script and an author of character design.

1.2.1 SANMAO'S STORY

The animation *Wanderings of Sanmao* (*Sanmao liulangji*), which premiered in 1958, might have been a capstone for the second generation of *manhua* artists, and a summary of their achievements in subversive criticism, artistic war efforts, and establishment of aesthetical conventions and communication codes of the new medium. Nevertheless, it is difficult to locate *Wanderings of Sanmao* in the canon of Chinese animation. It might be argued that the nostalgic and somewhat sentimental aura of past *manhua* styles detectable in this puppet film did not have potential to overtake the collective imagination of the society forging their new identity and aspirations in the reality of a rapid industrialization of the Great Leap Forward era.[2]

Sanmao is a homeless boy straying around the streets of Shanghai; an orphaned beggar who preserves cheerfulness and kindness of heart despite hunger, loneliness, and misery which he observes in the closest surroundings and experiences firsthand.

The readers of the comic books loved Sanmao's character design – this tall, thin boy had intelligent and amiable eyes, and above all, a characteristic 'hair style', i.e., three hair strings (his name literally means 'three hairs') freely floating around the top of his head. The first issue of *Sanmao* comic book was published on November 20, 1935, in the *Xiaochenbao* magazine. The humorous story pointed the readers' attention to the problem of social injustice and generated heavily emotional reactions.[3] During World War II, Sanmao 'enlisted' in the army (*Sanmao congjunji* was printed in the *Shenbao* magazine); the graphic stories of the period became quite brutal when depicting Sanmao's bayonet charges or tearing the enemies to shreds with grenades. The animated film's source material, the series *Wanderings of Sanmao*, was published in *Dagongbao* in 1947.[4] The plot of the comic returns to the Shanghai streets, but the pre-war satire transformed into a bitter, sometimes even hopeless, condemnation of a corrupted and cruel Kuomintang power apparatus. As Mary Ann Farquhar emphasizes, among characteristic motifs of Zhang Leping's work (contemporary themes, controversies, educational qualities, consideration for the living conditions of the masses), *Wanderings of Sanmao* series expose a new trope, i.e., "clear differentiation of class" (151). Xue Yanping builds an argument about Zhang's increasing frustration and anger that would strengthen his social world view. Xue finds Zhang's personal account about one 1947 winter night as a direct inspiration for creating *Wanderings …*; the researcher recalls the situation when Zhang, who was on his way home, noticed three barefoot children sitting on the pavement. Passing by the same place the next morning, the artist saw two dead little bodies. The overwhelming powerlessness and feeling of guilt forced him to return to Sanmao character, and accuse Kuomintang government of various wrongdoings (see Xue 108). The comics about Sanmao were also published in New China. Under new conditions, the social criticism made room for education, while the misery of wanderings was replaced with a passion for exploring an ever-changing world.

Zhang Leping and Zhang Chaoqun's script faithfully transposes the most moving contents of the *Wanderings of Sanmao* comics. Voice-over, a means of expression typical for classic Chinese animation, introduces the viewers to the filmic reality. This way one learns immediately that all the depicted injustices do not appear in New China, and the film's only aspiration is to build an understanding about the past. The time framework of the story is indicated in the most general terms: "Sanmao is a bitter child from the old society". Given the fact that the Kuomintang police, Chinese bourgeoise, and American soldiers function as villains, the action must be set between 1945 and 1949.

1.2.2 ANIMATED VARIANT OF FICTIONAL REALISM

Before being informed about the historical background, the viewers are presented with an impressive urban landscape: advertising banners hanging from the skyscrapers expose imported goods and pictures of women in negligees; blurry car and neon lights shine through the rain. The atmosphere of these images evokes an eroticized, modern graphic art of the *manhua*'s golden age (1920s–1930s).[5] Made for both commercial and artistic purposes, it is considered to commence the Chinese visual revolution of the late 1920s. Following sequences can be characterized by the high level of realism that gives grounds for arguing that Zhang Chaoqun and Zhang Leping's work may be called an animated variant of a fictional realism. This model, conceived in Hollywood, was also operational within the frames of social and socialist realism of Chinese live-action cinema from the 1930s to the 1950s. Jason McGrath lists the most significant indicators of this trend:

> continuity editing to smoothly organize time and space, the optical positioning of the spectator as an 'invisible observer' rather than an acknowledged addressee, and generally the deployment of cinematic techniques to

> encourage diegetic immersion in a plausible, mimetic fictional world, rather than to self-consciously draw attention to the act of cinematic narration itself (with a number of exceptions, such as beginning and ending credits, intertitles, nondiegetic musical scores, and so on).
>
> (358)

Animated *Wanderings of Sanmao* is dominated by the static takes which realistically present urban scenography in full or medium shots. A fixed point of view enables the depth of field as the most frequent filming locations are crossroads, corners, nooks, and courtyards. The props as well as scenography details were created with a consideration for diversity and authenticity what reinforces verisimilitude quality of the time-space filmic reality. Most often the puppets are shot in close-ups what reveals particular characteristics of the protagonists. The character design is individualized (facial structure and expression); each of over twenty puppets appearing in the film has their own posture, walking manner, and body language. Illustrative music score suppresses lack of sound effects related to the authentic urban life. Music compositions are grounded in keys and conventions of the Western music, and in the final scenes the viewers can also hear jazz – eventually, they are wandering around the streets of 'old Shanghai'. The ideological ambiguity of the animated *Wanderings of Sanmao* appears to be correlated with the wider phenomenon of an equivocal perception of the pre-war Shanghai culture. On the one hand, Zhang Chaoqun and Zhang Leping's film conveys contents substantial for the ideological identity of New China; on the other, its textual layer is strongly nostalgic, lyrical, and even sentimental. This said, the animated adaptation does not generate longing for the historical moment it depicts. Rather it evokes yearning for the forms of expression which allowed to speak up for the oppressed at those particular times.

1.2.3 TRANSCULTURAL PERSPECTIVE ON CHINESE ANIMATION'S ROOTS

The research on Shanghai *manhua* tradition is dominated by three overlapping perspectives: historical,[6] aesthetic,[7] and transcultural.[8] The proponents of the first two approaches concentrate on the works of national arts which internalized the modernist tendencies that were recurring globally, and electrifying artistic and intelligentsia *milieu* all around the world in the first half of the 20th century. The transcultural perspective locates the core of the reflection within the processes of an intercultural exchange. Martina Caschera acknowledges the systemic complexity of the 20th century satirical journalism developed in the course of cultural exchanges; she writes: "approaching cartoons as national autoimages enables us to further understand to what extent the 'Other' was involved in the modern process of discursive self-definition" (86). Thus, the transcultural paradigm in *manhua* studies reconstructs the aims and methods of artistic practices that complied with the specifics of the Chinese culture and led to the internalization of the modernist tendencies (among them, methods of cultural translation of the ideological discourses). These perspectives should not be understood as exclusive; only aggregating the conclusions enables the 'mapping' of aesthetic and ideological drifts of *manhua* – an essentially Chinese form of visual expression whose development was simultaneously conditioned by an intellectual and ideological turn towards nationalism, aesthetic syncretism, and specific internationalism.

Labeling *manhua* as an 'essentially Chinese form of visual expression' acknowledges a generic diversity of graphic narratives originating from the popular culture of the imperial China. The term *manhua* was adapted from the Japanese language (*manga*), and as most of the sources indicate, it came into use in the mid-1920s. The term denotes comic art, cartoons, and sketches with political and social angle, singular or multiplied, humorous comic strips printed in the press. The term *xinmanhua* denotes stories printed in the periodicals that were serialized or completed in one issue. *Lianhuanhua*, the so-called linked pictures, is a palm-size book telling one story with one image per page, such prints were produced under similar conditions as comic books. Woodcuts, traditional for the folk art (*banhua*) as well as new year's imagery (*nianhua*) have incorporated the themes and conventions of *manhua* along with the process of a progressing radicalization of the social life in China.[9] The reprints of the works of politically and socially engaged Western painters and caricature artists (e.g., Francisco Goya, Miguel Covarrubias, Georg Grosz, David Low) as well popularization of Japanese graphic art (due to Feng Zikai's efforts) have fundamentally strengthened modernist tendencies within narrative graphic art in China. As John A. Crespi writes:

> One can argue, then, that as a linguistically split term, manhua/sketch points not simply to the genre of the cartoon per se, but also to a 'visual emporium of cosmopolitanism' to be found in Republican-era Shanghai pictorials.
>
> (CRESPI, *BEYOND SATIRE* 225)

What is more, Crespi acknowledges an intermedia multiformity accepted within the *manhua* frames: the popular magazines would print ink drawings, true as well as faux woodcuts, cut-outs, photocollages, miniature graphic sculptures, and even diorama.[10] However, avant-garde, experimental, and diverse *manhua* works were inherently (generically or thematically) rooted in Chinese cultural experiences.

The first magazines publishing graphic satire emerged in the second half of the 19th century. Since 1918, when the first issue of *Shanghai Puck* (*Shanghai po ke*) was released, the popular graphics have started to absorb political and social awareness. Shen Bochen (editor-in-chief and highly productive artist who passed away prematurely in 1919) stated its mission in the 1918 editorial:

> first, to give advice and warning to both governments of the south and the north, and spur them to work in concerted efforts to create a unified government; second, to let Westerners understand Chinese culture and customs; and third, to promote the new morality and practices and discard the old.
>
> (SHEN 1–2, QTD. IN LENT AND XU 11)

So defined goals of the new magazine referred to the principles of the New Culture Movement as well as argumentation presented on the pages of the *New Youth* magazine. The authors collaborating with this opinion-making outlet set the foundations of the salvation movement ideology. Among the most important postulates, they called for a turn towards low culture in order to construct a unified identification pattern that would function as a common denominator for a stratified nation. At the same time, this new art would provide a communication platform shared by rebellious elites and peasantry (a group acknowledged as the only potential agent of a mass socio-political revolt).

At that time, Shanghai, as one of the most vital world metropolises, had become a center of liberal and left-wing thought. The urban bourgeoisie grew rapidly. On the one hand, numerous representatives of upper middle class from Europe, America, and Japan would multiply their resources with the means of the concessions and favorable trade conditions, on the other, the Chinese natives ascended into this group. Chinese bourgeoisie overcoming colonial social order was not stopped in their aspirations even at the dawn of the 1911 revolution when the state system disintegrated, and the power relations were overtaken either by the local representatives of the Chinese Republic or by the so-called warlords. Bourgeoisie thrived further regardless of the intensification of the conflict between Kuomintang and the Communist Party of China (CPC). The dynamics of the struggle between the parties was dictated by the following attempts and failures in constructing national unity fronts, brutal repressions, persecutions, assaults, and assassinations of the political opponents. But Shanghai in the 1920s was roaring. Consumption of good and entertainment was increasing, and the urban citizens have been undergoing processes of emancipation. New intelligentsia (recruiting either from the newly established Chinese national universities and missionary schools or the groups of emigrants returning from the study abroad in Japan, Europe, and the United States) vigorously agitated for cutting away from the neo-Confucian model of social organization with the means of technological development, mass (press-based) communication, and education.

The Shanghai Massacre of 1927, persecutions and executions of the communists, nominal unification of China under Chiang Kai-shek's rule, and moving the capital to Nanjing in 1928 gave the revolted youth a strong impulse to engage more deeply with Marxist–Leninist doctrine. The Soviet Union supported the CPC which was forced to play a defense game at that moment. Moscow performed various pro-Chinese political gestures and propaganda activities, among them animation production. *China in Flames* (*Kitaj w ognie, ruki procz ot Kitaja! / Китай в огне, руки прочь от Китая!*) run in the Soviet cinemas in 1925. The film made in mixed techniques (cut-out, hand-drawn) called for international solidarity with the Chinese people oppressed by the American imperialists, Western missionaries, and corrupted Chinese national governing party. The film directed by Nikolay Khodataev, Zenon Komissarenko, and Youry Merkulov was an unquestionable artistic achievement, even if the production was of a clearly propagandistic agenda. The film is overwhelmed with pathos of a monumental five-arm-star symbolics (and USSR holds a rank of an 'older brother' in ideological hierarchy), nevertheless, one cannot overlook the artistic subtlety of the image compositions. The animated depictions of the Chinese provinces reinterpret aesthetics of traditional landscape painting. Character design is mostly based on exaggerated caricature but once the faces of the oppressed Chinese men and women come into the picture, the shivering sensations appear as the viewer is forced to look directly onto transcending, androgynous visages of the people suffering. Meanwhile, the freedom of expression accessible for the Chinese artists and intellectuals was gradually yet radically limited.[11] The general atmosphere was soaked in far-reaching ideological polarization. Further concessions for the global powers, the more and more apparent threat of Japanese militarism, increasing social stratification, and overwhelming helplessness of individuals facing power apparatus, pushed the revolted elites to radically demand restoration of Sun Yat-sen's three principles – nationalism (*minzu*), democracy (*minzhu*), and welfare rights (*minsheng*). More frequently than ever, these demands incorporated calls for a revolution, bloody if needed.

1.2.4 VISUAL LANGUAGE OF THE NATIONAL SALVATION MOVEMENT

Among several *manhua* magazines published in the 1930s, the readership mostly appreciated *Shanghai Sketch* (*Shanghai manhua*, 1928–1930), *Modern Sketch* (*Shidai manhua*, 1934–1936), and *Independent Sketch* (*Duli manhua*, 1935–1936). Usually, the graphic artists were simultaneously commissioned by a few editorial offices, and at the same time, they collaborated on organizing work in the fields of arts and politics. The publishing houses were often shut down, mostly because of top-down procured financial troubles. If the early *manhua* satire aimed largely at constructive social criticism, the dominant tone of the 1930s became rather accusatory. The graphic art of the period condemned an omnipresent corruption (anti-Kuomintang contents), humiliating position of women in the society, child abuse, poverty in the rural areas (anti-feudal contents), misery experienced by the proletariat (anti-capitalist contents), low morale of the foreigners (anti-imperialist contents), Japanese militarism (anti-Japanese contents); all these motifs adding up to a wide imaginary of a nation's decline.[12]

In 1937, Zhang Ding's graphic work entitled *Victims of Famine Lie Dead in the Wilderness (The Scenery of Central Sichuan)* was published on the cover of *Modern Sketch*. Horrifying in its meaning and aesthetically borrowing from expressionism, the design captivates the viewer's attention through an empty gaze of an emaciated man who tries to stand still on the burned ground. Yet, something is pulling him down. It is a hungry child, crying and snuggling around the man's leg. In the background we see a skeleton; in-between the characters there is a broken doorframe with an imprinted new year's blessing: "deep and fulfilling blessings of the emperor". The motif of children's extreme suffering frequently appeared in the *manhua* strips; it is the main departure point of all the comics in the *Sanmao* series. The animators could not allow themselves for such a directness as depicted in Zhang Ding's work from 1937 or original Zhang Leping's comics. 1950s animated film served youth and children who were not supposed to be witnessing such an overt oppression on the cinema screens.

In one of the initial scenes, a hungry Sanmao shares his meal with a newly acquainted group of equally stray but younger kids. Unlike the protagonist, the kids have a guardian; however, this old and starving man literally puts them on sale, he says: "We have no food, we're all going to die if I don't sell them". This gives Sanmao an idea to put himself on market, and he writes a price on a cardboard: 10,000 yuan. Almost immediately he understands that the rich citizens of Shanghai prefer buying their kids a toy several times more expensive than to help out a living boy. In a manner which is characteristic for Zhang Leping, an extreme existential situation (Sanmao discovers that the children can be sold) is counter-balanced with a humorous situation (Sanmao discovers that selling himself will not ensure the profits). Zhang Leping turns his anger from the past decade into positive postulates: the new power relations and the new culture have to protect the most vulnerable members of the society (children) from the death of starvation and coldness; they must teach them how to write and read; they cannot allow children's working beyond their strength. In *Wanderings of Sanmao*, this humanitarian sensitivity dominates over the film's ideological didactics. This justifies speaking of Zhang Chaoqun and Zhang Leping's work not only in terms of direct agitation but rather as an expression of bitter lessons derived from the recent past.

Patriotic turn and new trends in arts resonated with the masses because of the employed conventions of realism and focus on politically and socially engaged themes. The involved artists appeared credible to the receivers since they were engaged in patriotic associations, societies, and informal groups, proving their viewpoint with an action. When in 1937, the Japanese Imperial Army invaded wide parts of China, and introduced regulations of a racist, exterminating dictatorship, the artists formed the National Salvation Cartoon Propaganda Corps under the auspices of the national party (KMT). The corps were a publisher of the magazines: *National Salvation Cartoons* (*Jiuwang manhua*) and *Resistance of War Cartoons* (*Kangzhan manhua*); several other national salvation *mahua* outlets also emerged. These small military formations (the two groups led by the artists-soldiers, Te Wei and Zhang Leping, counted 100 fully available members in 1945) turned out to be extraordinarily active, effective, and mobile.[13] The corps were officially dissolved in 1940 (KMT leadership was afraid of the communist infiltration); up until that moment, they have organized over 100 exhibitions at various places between Shanghai, Hankou, Guangzhou, Hong Kong, Guilin, Chongqing, Wuhan, Changsha, and Nanjing. After 1940, many of the corps' members crossed over to the bases in Yan'an where they continued their artistic struggle.

The very term 'exhibition' does not reflect the whole spectrum of the *manhua* corps' activities conducted at the frontlines. In addition to regular exhibiting of art works, the corps' members significantly intensified and transformed methods of propaganda work known from the USSR:

> From 1937 to 1945, in fact, cartoons, like spoken dramas, were more than an art form: they were an effective

> educational tool and a potent agent for political indoctrination. They also served as a major chronicle of the age, bearing witness to a devastating conflict. Of all forms of propaganda, the cartoon can be the most persuasive.
>
> (HUNG 94)

Thousands of *manhua* works were exposed daily on the posters hanging at the city walls, banners held by the marching soldiers, scrolls rolled and unrolled during the performances of the akin theatrical brigades. The exhibitions of the drawings were accompanied with the addresses of the agitators who were reporting and explaining the current war situation. The fighters from the artistic propaganda corps reached out to the inhabitants of the frontlines and beyond. Intense and continuous work of the graphic designers caught an attention of the CPC's decision-makers and boosted the significance of *manhua* in an overall propaganda system.

The rhetoric and stylistics of a war-time *manhua* have fostered several representative tropes and figures enabling the receivers to immediately decode stories of ugly traitors (*hanjian*), brutal Japanese occupants, heroic and supportive soldiers of the People's Liberation Army (PLA). The symbolic language of a pre-war *manhua* relied on anthropomorphism (e.g., pigs and monkeys denoted the quislings; snakes and vipers represented the threats awaiting behind the Great Wall; etc.), historicization (contemporary politicians appearing in disguise of the historical traitors), caricature (presenting the wide national groups with the means of caricatural representation of their leaders), and stereotypization (e.g., attributes of the Japanese characters were glasses, mustache, buck teeth; Chinese traitors were unhealthily obese or thin with an unsightly visage; the imperialist-Westerners had long noses, light hair, etc.). In the mid-1930s, such representations maintained the features of grotesque exaggeration that would ridicule and belittle specific social situations and villainous public persons. Patriotic emphasis of the war-time *manhua* underlined brutality when referring to both, the disgraceful actions of the enemies (executions, rapes) and heroic deeds of the rightful masses. There is an observable shift towards the aesthetic paradigm of a romanticist, revolutionary realism.[14]

In the narrative graphic art of the Civil War period, the concerns of inflation, hunger, prostitution, human trafficking, and official corruption became a casebook of inspirational themes. On the layer of figurative representation, the emperor Hirohito became replaced by Chiang Kai-shek, while the American military substituted the Japanese Imperial Army. Animated *Wanderings of Sanmao* presents a typical set of negative characters: a long-nose American soldier beats the boy and robs him; Sanmao constantly fights and outsmarts the clumsy Kuomintang militia as well as their outsized and servile collaborators. The impious villains are grotesque, hideous, and unintelligent. The film denounces brutality; it rather seems to revoke a pre-military *manhua* when the enemies, representatives of evil and injustice, were not yet a subject of dehumanization.

1.2.5 SEARCHING FOR UNITY, FINDING NOSTALGIA

Animated *Wanderings of Sanmao* corresponds with a line of alarmistic *manhua*, while themes of a nationalistic agitation against the enemy are rather absent in its textual layer. If the previously discussed *The Emperor's Dream* suppressed the need to visualize a heroic side, then in *Wanderings of Sanmao*, the viewers observe a counter process. Militia, exploiters, American soldiers, etc., they all bring chaos to Sanmao's life. But the most important interactions occur between the boy and the other paupers – his comrades in misery. In some regard, Zhang Leping and Zhang Chaoqun's film turns towards the genre of psychological drama, especially in the scenes when Sanmao interacts with other children (importantly, he builds up a friendship with an illiterate child Aijin). The economic oppression is the most important frontline of Sanmao's daily struggles. All the positive characters fight to preserve their dignity in the urban jungle subjected to the needs of imperialists and the desires of the hedonists. Their efforts may be successful only if the most miserable of the proletariat will compassionately open up to each other, thus unifying in their resistance. In the final scenes, Sanmao struggles with a drunk American and Kuomintang policeman. A supposedly highly symbolic scene of the KMT's sun-badge falling into a sewer does not release an emotional culmination. The joyful fulfillment appears only with the image of Sanmao and Aijin's smiling faces. They were beaten and robbed, their working place was devasted, but together they managed to take revenge on the brutal power force. Recalling modernist spirit and people's democracy ideas, this film wanders away from an ideological radicalism of Mao Zedong Thought which in the end of the 1950s established the policies of the Anti-Rightist Campaign and the Great Leap Forward.

Sanmao is a fascinating character – he emerges trustful, cheerful, and light-hearted from all the miserable adventures. One finds a deposit of lyricism and fictional sentimentalism on this layer and acknowledges Zhang Leping's nostalgia for modernist *manhua* as the major referential point of the analysis. It is observable within the narrative and formal strategies employed in the creation of textual/visual body of the film. However, if we look at the film through the prism of an artistic persona of the director, Zhang Chaoqun, the presence of a nostalgic charm within it may be also related to the international context of the puppet film aesthetics of the period.

Zhang Leping's influence on the creative process behind filming the animated *Wanderings of Sanmao* cannot be overestimated, but at the same time the role of Zhang Chaoqun – the director, cinematographer, and co-writer of this production – should be acknowledged too. Zhang began his film career in 1950 as a cinematographer in live-action production *Peace Pigeon* (*Hepingge*, dir. Tao Jin) (Xue 111). At that film set Zhang met Jin Xi, an artist who holds a position in the history of Chinese animation comparable only with Wan Laiming, Te Wei, or A Da. Until 1960, Zhang

Chaoqun collaborated on seventeen animation productions – ten out of them were directed or co-directed by Jin Xi (Xue 111–112). Jin and Zhang worked together on the most famous puppet film of the 1950s, *The Magic Brush* (*Shenbi*). One may assume that as one of Jin Xi's close collaborators, Zhang Chaoqun at some point was confronted with the aesthetic and intellectual convictions argued by the master of the Chinese puppet animation.

In Jin Xi's rich theoretical output, the concept of *xieyin* ("puns and parables") should be closely studied. *Xieyin* denotes such a mode of storytelling (textual and audio/visual alike) where the fantasy masks the reality with the use of anthropomorphism, caricature, and exaggeration. It does so in order to comment on the reality (see Macdonald 164). Such attitude is also characteristic of Jiří Trnka, the Czechoslovak master of European puppet film whose studio Jin Xi visited during his trip to Karlovy Vary and Prague in 1954.[15] It seems possible that Jin Xi became fascinated with a phantasmagorical aura of Trnka's *The Emperor's Nightingale* (*Císa ův slavík*, 1949) or with a daring parody of a Hollywood Western movie *Arie Preriae* (1949), he even might have seen preparations for the production of the famous *The Good Soldier Švejk* (*Dobrý voják Švejk*, 1954). Paweł Sitkiewicz speaks of a specific style of the Czech master who has influenced the aesthetic approach of Jin Xi: "he found a golden mean between the cosmopolitism of a universal art which speaks to the viewers all around the world, and the uniqueness of a national art, deeply rooted in the local tradition and history" (Sitkiewicz 93). Furthermore, Sitkiewicz recalls the words of Trnka who himself was a student of the famous Josef Skupa (a ground-breaking innovator of the Czech satirical, puppet theater of the 20th century): "Puppet films are efficient not only in the fields of caricature and satire, but they also work for the immensely lyrical stories and the ones whose themes require presenting an emotional fervor" (Broz 20, qtd. in Sitkiewicz 95).

The 'Czech lessons' which Jin Xi has shared with the readers of the literature and film magazines upon his return to China (see

Macdonald, 2017), and propagated among his artistic collaborators, were supposed to help the puppet film authors to reconcile the ideological demands with inherent lyrical atmosphere of this film form. Puppet films are prone to generate fantastical narrative situations and activate subtlety in the use of symbols and visual metaphors. *The Magic Brush*, which takes place in 'once-upon-a-time feudal China' was highly successful with audiences as well as cinema and culture officials. Animated *Wanderings of Sanmao* became neither a success nor a subject of criticism. In the spirit of Jin Xi's theories, the creators of the animated *Wanderings of Sanmao* transferred aura and poetics of a cordial fairytale into recognizable, visual, and ideological discourses. Extending Jin Xi's ideas, they referred to the symbolic reservoir directly related to the recent events in China's political and cultural history. Detectable nostalgic tones did not coincide with the film's contemporary social and ideological atmosphere which was already infused with the revolutionary, industrial fervor. Loyal to the principle of an ideological compliance, the artists did not idealize the tokens of the bygone era. Viewed from the time and cultural distance, this film appears as a compelling example of a unique feature of Chinese classic animation, i.e., artistic and intellectual inseparability of animation and comics arts.

NOTES

1. Te Wei said, "I like animation but I didn't like to do production. I liked doing cartoons, not all those monotonous frames. But it was an order and I had to do this job" (Lent and Xu, *Te Wei and Chinese Animation*).
2. The Great Leap Forward (1958–1962) was a globally unprecedented industrial modernization campaign conducted accordingly to the line of 'going all out, aiming high, and achieving more, faster and more economical results', aimed at getting ahead of British economic production in fifteen years. Among other movements, it embraced accelerated collectivization of the countryside (assembling mass communes which replaced households and constituted new administrative units), water-conservancy campaign, steel production campaign. The individuals were turned into subjects of

mass, exhausting, and drastically underpaid labor force. Centrally planned phases of the campaign did not account for natural specifics of the land cultivation, and imposed unrealistic requirements on the working masses. The death causalities grew in the period of the Great Famine resulting from agricultural mismanagement (November 1958–January 1962). Great Leap Forward was designed by Mao Zedong himself. Regardless of inner tensions within the Party (with their peak in July 1959), formal investigations into the catastrophe (1960–1961), and denouncement of the wrong policies in January 1962 (during the enlarged party gathering in Beijing Liu Shaoqi named the famine as a man-made disaster), the Chairman had never been held accountable for this tragedy. See Dikötter, 2017.

3. The editorial office was flooded with the letters of compassion and charity goods for the homeless boy (Lent and Xu, *Comics Art in China* 26).
4. Sanmao of the Civil War period made a notable cinematic appearance in a live-action adaptation *Wanderings of Three Hairs the Orphan* (*Sanmao liulang ji*, 1949, dir. Zhao Ming, Yan Gong). The film resonates with the then globally universal tendencies of neorealistic cinema by exposing themes of children's misery and involving scenes shot on location. The titular character played by Wang Longji seems bolder than his animated version from the late 1950s; similarly, the overall tone of the film is much more gruesome than the animated adaptation regardless of certain elements of comedy and the final sequence presenting the PLA's victory parade in Shanghai in May 1949.
5. For example, Zhang Guangyu, *Degeneracy* (*Duoluo*), *Shanghai Sketch*, November 21, 1929 (see Crespi, *China's Modern Sketch* 16).
6. See Hung, 1994; *Asian Popular Culture* 1995, *Themes and Issues in Asian Cartooning*, 1999; *Illustrating Asia*, 2011; Lent and Xu, 2017.
7. See Crespi, 2015, 2021; Landsberger, 2002, and his curated website chineseposters.net.
8. See Bevan, 2015; Caschera, 2018.
9. See Lent and Xu, *Comics Art in China* XII.
10. The diorama form is called *mandiao*, Crespi describes it as following: "These miniatures were reminiscent of the traditional handicraft art of clay figurines, but may also have been inspired by the puppet-like 'personettes' invented in the 1930s by American cartoonist and commercial artist Russell Patterson for use in fashion advertising and Hollywood films" (*China's Modern Sketch* 73).

11. The Republic of China's Film Censorship Committee evaluated production in regard to the possible offensive and superstitious contents, and from 1931, it has also opposed films that would critically portray social issues or use local dialects instead of an official Mandarin one. See *Cinema and Urban Culture in Shanghai, 1922-1943*; Johnson, 2008; Teo, 2010; *A Companion to Chinese Cinema*; Lent and Xu, 2017.
12. Following *manhua* works appear representative for the discussed tendencies: Gao Longsheng, *United*, (*Yuebao*, March 15, 1937; see Hung 108); Ye Qianyu, *The Secret to Raising Money* (*Modern Sketch*, February, 1934; see Crespi *China's Modern Sketch* 18); Wang Zhu, *Illustrated Biography of a Child Prostitute* (*Modern Sketch*, 1934–1937; see Crespi *China's Modern Sketch* 51); Ye Qianyu, *Flower of Society* (*Shanghai Sketch*, August 11, 1928; see Crespi *China's Modern Sketch* 18); Liu Xinquan, *The West Wind Creeps East* (drawing from Hong Kong, 1930s; see Crespi *China's Modern Sketch* 47); Chen Juanyin, *Viewing the Sunrise over the East China Sea* (*Modern Sketch*, 1936; see Crespi *China's Modern Sketch* 39).
13. Te Wei wrote in 1938: "I'm on the go from 8am to 5pm editing *Mobilization Pictorial* under the Military Training Association, and sometimes work at home till midnight. I greatly admire the spirit of Lu Shaofei. On top of editing *Mobilization*, the two of us design book and magazine covers while contributing regularly to *Salvation Daily*, *National Survival*, and *The New Front*" (22).
14. The following works are representative: Feng Zikai, *Bombing* (*Hongzha*, 1937); Li Keran (*Killing Contest*, *Wenyi zhendi*, January 1, 1939; see Hung 102); Chen Yanqiao, *Our Vanguard* (*Resistance Sketch*, 6–7); Li Hua, *Bound China Has Roared* (*Resistance Sketch*, 6–7).
15. Xue Yanping ascertains that Jin Xi was the first Chinese animator to conduct a study visit abroad (see Xue 309).

REFERENCES

A Companion to Chinese Cinema, edited by Yingjin Zhang Yingjin, John Wiley Blackwell Publishing, 2012 (especially chapters: *History and Geography*, pp. 23-150; *Industry and Institution*, pp. 151-262).

Asian Comics, edited by John A. Lent, University Press of Mississippi, 2015.

Asian Popular Culture, edited by John A. Lent, Westview Press, 1995.

Bevan, Paul. *A Modern Miscellany: Shanghai Cartoon Artists, Shao Xunmei's Circle, and the Travels of Jack Chen, 1926–1938*. Brill, 2015.

Caschera, Martina, "Chinese Modern Cartoon. A transcultural approach to Modern Sketch." *Altre Modernità*, vol. 2, no. 2, 2018, pp. 85–103.

Cinema and Urban Culture in Shanghai, 1922–1943, edited by Yingjin Zhang, Stanford University Press, 1999.

Crespi, John A. "Beyond Satire: The Pictorial Imagination of Zhang Guangyu's 1945 *Journey to the West* in Cartoons." *The Oxford Handbook of Modern Chinese Literatures*, edited by Carlos Rojas, Andrea Bachner, Oxford University Press, 2015, pp. 215–240.

Crespi, John A. "China's Modern Sketch - 1. The Golden Era of Cartoon Art, 1934–1937." *MIT Visualizing Cultures*, 2011, visualizingcultures.mit.edu/modern_sketch/ms_essay01.html. Accessed 20 Oct 2021.

Dikötter, Frank. *Mao's Great Famine: The History of China's Most Devastating Catastrophe, 1958–62*. 2010. Bloomsbury, 2017.

Farquhar, Mary Ann. "*Sanmao*: Classic Cartoons and Chinese Popular Culture." *Asian Popular Culture*, edited by John A. Lent, Westview Press, 1995, pp. 139–158.

Hung, Chang-tai. *War and Popular Culture. Resistance in Modern China, 1937–1945*. University of California Press, 1994.

Illustrating Asia. Comics, Humour Magazines, and Picture Books, edited by John A. Lent, University of Hawaii Press, 2011.

Johnson, Matthew, David. *International and Wartime Origins of the Propaganda State: The Motion Picture in China, 1897–1955*. 2008. University of California, PhD dissertation.

Landsberger, Stefan. "The Deification of Mao: Religious Imagery and Practices During the Cultural Revolution and Beyond." *China's Great Proletarian Cultural Revolution: Master Narratives and Post-Mao Counternarratives*, edited by Woei Lien Chong, Rowman & Littlefield Publishers, 2002, pp. 139–184.

Lent, John A., Xu, Ying, *Comics Art in China*. University Press of Mississippi, 2017.

Lent, John A., Xu, Ying. "Te Wei and Chinese Animation: Inseparable, Incomparable." *Animation World Magazine*, 15 Mar 2002, awn.com/animationworld/te-wei-and-chinese-animation-inseparable-incomparable. Accessed 20 Oct 2021.

Macdonald, Sean. "Jin Xi: Master of puppet animation." *Journal of Chinese Cinemas*, vol. 11, no. 2, 2017, pp. 159–174.

McGrath, Jason. "Cultural Revolution Model Opera Films and the Realist Tradition in Chinese Cinema." *The Opera Quarterly*, vol. 26, no. 2–3, 2010, pp. 343–376.

Resistance Sketch, no. 3, 1938, p. 24, issuu.com/johncrespi/docs/resistance_sketch_e. Accessed 20 Oct 2021.

Shen Bochen. "Benkan de Zeren." ["The Responsibilities of the Magazine."] *Shanghai Puck*, no. 1, 1918, pp. 1–2.

Sitkiewicz, Paweł. *Polska szkoła animacji [Polish School of Animation]*. Gdańsk, słowo/obraz terytoria, 2011.

Te, Wei. "Cartoon News." *Resistance Sketch*, vol. 3, 1938, p. 22.

Teo, Stephen, "The Martial Arts Film in Chinese Cinema: Historicism and the National." *Art, Politics and Commerce in Chinese Cinema*, edited by Zhu Ying and Stanley Rosen, Hong Kong University Press, 2010, pp. 99–110.

Themes and Issues in Asian Cartooning: Cute, Cheap, Mad, and Sexy, edited by John A. Lent, Bowling Green State University Popular Press, 1999.

Xue, Yanping. *Zhongguo dingge donghua [Chinese stop motion]*. Communication University of China Press, 2014.

II

Calls of the Continuous Revolution, 1960s–1970s: Films of You Lei

CHAPTER 2.1

"To Live is to Serve the People"

Rooster Crows at Midnight

In the span of less than ten years between the two most (in)famous and darkest campaigns of the Maoist era, the Great Leap Forward (1958) and the Cultural Revolution (1966), a multitude of highly meaningful socio-political and cultural events occurred. *De facto* repudiation of the USSR/PRC strategic alliance (1958–1960) aggravated nationalistic tendencies. The rise of political tensions increased frequency of the oppressive practices such as struggle sessions and invigilation. On the other hand, there appeared a rising, yet unnamed, tide of retribution for the social and economic mistakes of the Great Leap Forward. Mao Zedong temporarily lost full control over the state power apparatus, while the 'pragmatists', led by Liu Shaoqi, Deng Xiaoping, and Zhou Enlai, initiated processes of reforms.[1] Indeed, the historians acknowledge Liu, Deng, and Zhou's experiments of that time as a 'draft' refined in the 1980s by Deng (Liu and Zhou have

DOI: 10.1201/9781003241607-6

not lived to see the full implementation of these plans).[2] A power play performed by the major actors on the main political stage have been reproducing itself across all layers of social organization, and only naturally it has not bypassed the 'culture front'. The cinema system's decision makers endorsed reformist movements what was held against them during the Cultural Revolution. Through the lenses of the film history research, tokens of the reformist approach emerge from the analysis of the official documents, examples of film criticism or theoretical writings, and the films themselves. The tendency for reducing an ideological disambiguation notably reveals itself when the production is examined against a wide background, accounting also for the films which have not renounced rhetoric of direct agitation. The management of the cinematography of this period appears as a mechanism of balancing between an ideological orthodoxy and intellectual, revisionist progression. In a way, this strategy replicates the *modus operandi* of the 'pragmatic faction' of the times. Caution in designing the outreach of the changes, graduality of their implementation, and solicitude for their logical validation within the frames of a dominant doctrine, characterized a relative relaxation of the early 1960s.

2.1.1 THE REVISIONISTS AND THE RADICALS

The film historians who reconstruct a trajectory of the political conflict determining this cultural history phase depart from the antagonism between the Ministry of Culture and the Party Shanghai Committee. The latter institution regulated the functioning of the film studios in the city. The feud was personified by the conflicted officials: Xia Yan (the Deputy Minister of Culture responsible for cinematography)[3] and Jiang Qing (Mao Zedong's spouse; the member of the advisory committee for cinematography at the Ministry of Culture whose partisans were the Shanghai's committee members).[4] In October 1961 (i.e., the point in the historical timeline when the 'pragmatic faction' led a more overt criticism of the Great Leap Forward, and by implication – an indirect criticism of Mao Zedong's leadership), Xia Yan published in the *Red Flag* (*Hongqi*) magazine the article *Raise Our Country's Film Art to a New Level.*[5] Paul G. Pickowicz recalls Xia's postulates built on the grounds of Marxism–Leninism:

> He complained that the artistic quality of most films was unacceptably low, the range of topics treated in motion pictures was woefully inadequate, and the cinematic forms employed were insufficiently diverse. The Great Leap Forward was nowhere mentioned, but he pointed out that films should not be produced in a hasty, assembly-line fashion; that it is unnecessary for every film to treat 'grave topics' of immediate economic and political concern; and that deeply rooted artistic traditions should not be indiscriminately abandoned in the rush to carry out the transition to socialism in the arts. Furthermore, he noted that sudden and sporadic bursts of energy and sheer 'enthusiasm' cannot make up for the absence of professional expertise and a detailed knowledge of the complexities of social life in the development of a viable film industry. The characters portrayed in films should not be one-dimensional abstractions whose only function is to convey the 'spirit of the times'.
>
> (214)

What is more, the filmmakers, who gathered around Xia Yan, were conspicuously successful in terms of artistic and viewership accomplishments, while the scholarly practice of historical and theoretical research opened up for modernization.[6]

Jiang Qing vigorously promoted two of Mao Zedong's directives about literature and arts (1961, 1963) which have counterbalanced the so-called 'Xia-Chen revisionist line'.[7] Jiang Qing's output as an actress and culture activist was thoroughly studied;[8] the established research indicates Jiang's perseverance in conceptualizing revolutionary art as well as overtaking the power mechanisms allowing for implementation of her concepts. Before Jiang Qing became a leader of the Central Culture Revolution Group in 1966 and formulated the thematic range and aesthetic model of the revolutionary artistic creation, her views on artistic expression as grounded in the anti-subjectivism and anti-criticism had been already consolidated. Jiang's writings, saturated with the ideological jargon, above all reveal a conviction that the art is essentially a device of social engineering for it attends to two major concerns: serving the masses and changing mass consciousness.[9] In this light, any reflection on the 'pre-communist' times (however critical it may be) is dispensable since it is doomed to represent a feudal world order. In Jiang's views, any manifestation of the 'bourgeois humanism' approach in the construction of the characters (even if they undergo a complete change in the course of story's development) contradicts the postulate of an absolute integrity of the characters' identity. A hero is determined by the unwavering, desired values of moral and ideological nature, while the villain may only become more overtly despicable. Until 1964, the film studios, Shanghai Animation Film Studio (SAFS) among them, attempted to adhere (to a possible and reasonable extent) to Xia Yan's ideas. At the same time, it seemed only pragmatic and strategic to initiate productions that could be welcomed by the radical faction.

2.1.2 YOU LEI: A DOGMATIC ANIMATOR

Among the creative cadres of the SAFS, it was puppet animator You Lei who had consistently adopted a radical, anti-revisionist approach in his films that fiercely and ruthlessly attacked all possible enemies of the people. His filmmaking style broke away from the static heritage of visual arts and unlocked the puppet film for cinematic qualities related to the movement within the frames, camera work, dynamic editing, and epic poetics of the image composition. Regardless of such qualitative improvements, the Chinese animation historians who have greatly contributed to the development of the discipline (e.g., John A. Lent and Xu Ying, Sean Macdonald, Xue Yanping, Daisy YanDu) do not present overviews of You Lei's work, even though his name reappears in their studies. This omission seems justified as a means of avoiding elevation in the canon of the filmmaker who, throughout his career, has overtly and continuously propagated and affirmed the most brutal aspects of the totalitarian regime. The following two chapters that examine You Lei's films do not attempt to revise his position in the historical studies of Chinese animation, but to understand means and methods with which animated art may so explicitly and organically comply with the darkest summons of the ideological doctrine.

You Lei's filmography, reconstructed here accordingly to online data bases (mtime; baike.baidu; movie.douban), consists of thirteen films he directed (among them two co-directed films, and one where he served as an assistant director; the first individual work was made in 1958), five productions in which he worked as an animator (debut in 1956), two in which he collaborated as a puppet and model designer (debut in 1955), and one in which he was a director of photography (1981). Available bio notes inform that You Lei started working at the SAFS in 1950 (transferred there from the Shanghai Puppet Theatre together with Yan Zheguang) and participated in over thirty productions. Since 1955, he has worked with the most acknowledged of the Shanghai animators – he created art projects for Yan Zheguang's *Mr Dongguo* (*Dongguo xiansheng*, 1955, co-dir. Xu Bingduo),[10] assisted Jin Xi on the set of *The Magic Brush*, animated puppets in Jin Xi's *Flaming Mountain Legend* (*Huo yan shan*, 1958) as well as feature-length *Peacock Princess* (*Kongque gongzhu*, 1963), he was also a puppet animator in the previously discussed *Wanderings of Sanmao*. Between 1958 and 1976 (i.e., during the rule of Mao Zedong), You Lei directed seven films (mostly of thirty- or forty-minute duration), all of them being direct and agitational illustrations of the intricacies of the dominant doctrine. *The Great Sparrow Campaign* (*Da maque*, 1958), as the very title suggests, tells an episode from the Four

Pests Campaign (*chusi hai*), its protagonists attempt to break a sparrow killing record. Courageous and attentive to the issues of animal welfare, the children from the rural commune are the main characters of *A Shepherd Boy* (*Muyang shaonian*, 1960). In the film *Chief Li Challenges the Cookhouse Squad* (*Li kezhang qiao nan chuishi ban*, 1965), the People's Liberation Army (PLA) soldiers equally seriously and passionately bring an order to the garrison's cantina, practice military drills, and study Mao Zedong Thought. *The Story of a Big Oar* (*Dalu de gushi*, 1976) takes place at the maritime front of the Civil War.

Rooster Crows at Midnight (1964) and *The Little 8th Route Army* (1973) remain the director's only works acknowledged by the international scholars and curators. These two You Lei's films constitute an inspiring material for the analysis conducted from the ideological criticism perspective. As in the previously mentioned titles, the protagonists are children who do not restrain from violence, and remain fascinated with the Communist Party of China. You Lei continued filmmaking career until the early 1990s when he had established several studios, and became involved in commercial projects addressing newly defined needs of a child audience of the opening-up and reforms era.

2.1.3 CONSTRUCTING HISTORY

The film *Rooster Crows at Midnight* may be acknowledged as an interesting exemplification of the Maoist culture production's inclination to remold the textual contents deeply rooted in the collective imagination in accordance with the inner flows and updates of the dominant doctrine. The creators of such culture texts as well as their receivers absorbed new, desired meanings, and 'forget' the hitherto recognized interpretations of the texts. The story about the malicious landlord, Zhou Bapi, and a young, clever field worker, Gao Yubao, presents a complex relationship between the historical reality and the fictional reality of the culture text. In 1951, the literary magazine of People's Liberation Army, *Jiefangjun wenyi*, published the memoirs of a young soldier named Gao Yubao. In a letter to the editors, he claimed to start working on this text in 1949 as he was willing to learn how to read and write. At that time, the soldier Gao was practically an analphabet therefore he was writing down his thoughts with the use of a few Chinese characters he knew, self-created pictograms, and drawings. Only later his colleagues and leaders would help the soldier to 'translate' the text into written Chinese language. Reminiscence of Gao's childhood was highly touching. Thirteen episodes from the life of a poor, peasant family were taking back the readers to the year of 1937; following traumatic events marked the plot's development: death of the loved ones, wartime wanderings, slave labor. Dream of education functioned as a leit-motif of this episodic narration. Gao Yubao's piece underwent several editorial reviews, and in longer or shorter variants, it was published by different magazines dedicated to promotion of socialist culture, loyalty towards the Party, and anti-feudal contents (publications from 1952, 1955, 1972). In 1964, You Lei adapted the memoires into an animated film. In 1970, the magazine *Chinese Literature* reprinted the film's script, while in 1973, Beijing-based Foreign Language Press released in English a specific form of *lianhuanhua* where the drawings were replaced with the stills from You's film.

Christine Jeanette Kleemeier presented the official publishing history of Gao Yubao's text in her MA thesis defended at the British Columbia University in 1981. Kleemeier critically analyzed the collected source material and added an annex with the translations of the selected editorial notes as well as the letter Gao Yubao wrote to the researcher. The famous autobiography of a soldier-analphabet requires rigidly critical analytical apparatus. The researchers convincingly undermine status of Gao Yubao as an analphabet and authenticity of the text since it went through numerous filters of editorial work. A close narrative kinship is established between Gao's autobiography and Mao Zedong's memoires as well as with Nikolai Ostrovsky's famous novel *How the Steel Was Tempered* (*Kak zakalyalas' stal'*, 1934). Eventually the status of Gao Yubao as an author became a subject of methodical verification (see Wu). Opening credits in You Lei's film mention Gao Yubao; however, the reprint of the script in 1970 replaces information about the author with a quotation from Mao Zedong. The 1973 publication does not mention any individual as a creator of the narrative.[11]

The concern of authorship attribution seems less convoluted than a changing trajectory of the text's ideological meanings trailing constantly modifying aims of the Maoist propaganda. This reflection departs from the notion that ideologically, Gao Yubao's memoires belong to the category of anti-feudal narrations. This large group consists of texts calling for the crackdown on neo-Confucian world order (traditions as well as superstitions regulating the public sphere and power hierarchy), but also empower women's emancipation and equal rights struggle, and demand distribution of land and goods among the groups deprived of property (above all, the peasantry). Patriotic agenda propagated by the Communist Party of China (CPC) well resonated with the groups of intelligentsia and bourgeoisie, but as Mao Zedong noticed, only the commitment and mass support of countrymen and women could have secured the communists' victory in an agrarian China. In the mid-20th century, the peasant class constituted approximately eighty percent of the whole society (*Key Papers on Chinese Economic History* xiv). For this reason, the first regulations executed by the communist officials on the territories overtaken during the war concerned the land reform. Propaganda clearly defined its causes (evil deeds of the landlords, repressiveness and injustice of the tax system), methods (distribution of wealth such as land, resources, field-labor products among the rural communities; liberation of the social frustration through the struggle sessions), and aims (the people overtake control of their own lives). In 1947, as the military success was progressing, the land reform gained traction and outreach. These efforts were crowned with the 1950 land reform legislation, and the collectivization of the Great Leap Forward campaign expanded this idea. Just after the new law was launched, Gao Yubao's memoires were published for the first time, and they perfectly accentuated the meanings of the introduced reform.

2.1.4 IDEOLOGICAL EXPRESSIVENESS: IMAGES-IDEAS

The protagonist of this unique biographical narrative experienced hardships of growing up in a poor, peasant family. Indebted, his folks sold him into slave labor. Extremely greedy Zhou Bapi beguiled the field workers to work long hours without a pay. The labor was extorted with yelling, beatings, and threats; eventually Zhou Bapi applied a pathetic trick – each night the landlord was sneaking into a henhouse, pretending to crow like a rooster, he was decoying the enslaved workers to get up and start working in the fields much before the day breaks. Young Gao saw Zhou Bapi's act and convinced the others to take a revenge. Allegedly saving the henhouse from a thief, the workers surrounded the shack an gave the landlord a thrashing. You Lei's film is a faithful adaptation of this well-known story.

The opening sequence presents field workers returning to their cottage at dusk, while the voice-over locates the storyline in the mythical time 'prior to the Liberation' ("During those dark days of old society, farmhands were suffering a lot from their landlords, there are so many cruel and twisted stories about how landlords exploit the poor, and here's one of them"). The scene cuts to the landlord's house interior, and we see Zhou Bapi and his wife sitting comfortably on the traditional bed-stove *kang*, plotting a cunning intrigue. The voice-over continues: "Look at his face! He's up to no good for sure!" Specific formal operations precede the call to look directly at the oppressor. The camera which follows the peasants on the route to their barracks stops just before they pass the gates, travels to the left, and zooms into the landlord's house through the window. After the cut, we see the Zhou couple looking out from the very same window the camera traversed through. It approaches the puppets, and closes-up on Zhou Bapi's visage exactly in time of voice-over commending: "Look!" Camera movement consistently generates an impression of a close observation. Close-ups and zooms are typical for You Lei's style. Importantly, regardless of the voyeuristic motifs playing a significant role in the plot's development, the director positions the viewer as a witness rather than a peeper.

The character design clearly communicates personality of the protagonists. To some extent, the usefulness of propaganda relies on generating an immediate recognition of a given individuality as a particular representative of a wide network of ideological meanings. In the models of Ms. and Mr. Zhou puppets, the designers applied a comical size contrast between the characters. A slim figure of Zhou Bapi echoes Chiang Kai-shek's puppet from *The Emperor's Dream*, while the figure of a wife is short and corpulent, her face is pale and swollen. The puppets are deprived of a changing facial expression. Zhou Bapi is ominously tight-lipped, his wife's eyes remain squint, her mouth half-opened. Whenever set in motion, they move bow-legged in an ungainly manner. Zhou Bapi either walks with a stick or crawls on the ground, he also constantly coughs. All these features clearly suggest viciousness and degeneration. The modeling and movement of the positive characters reveal completely opposite qualities. Recurrent close-ups on their faces (and especially, on the eyes) expose a monumental strength, fortitude, firmness, and pride. A plodding movement or a sweat dripping off on their faces represent a condition of a heavy physical fatigue. Even if tired, the field workers appear prevailing. Their (puppet) bodies are well built, healthy, strong. The character design in You Lei's film follows the rudiments of the Maoist propaganda stylistics. Image-ideas bestow a concrete expression upon abstract political and social concepts. As Stefan Landsberger emphasized such operation became a predominant communicative convention since the majority of the propaganda receivers of the visual communication in the 1940s and the 1950s were illiterates (*The Chinese Art of Propaganda* 11). You Lei exercised this strategy to its fullest extent in *The Little 8th Route Army*.

Evilness imprinted in Zhou Bapi's figure originates from the Maoist definition of the features characteristic of the owners' class, determined by moral decay, depravation, and almost genetic inclination to violence. As such, it represents a phenomenon appearing on the border of constructing collective imagination and collective historical memory. Wu Gao discusses a historical process of 'constructing bad reputation' of the feudal lords. He locates this process in the Maoist discourse of history in regard to three characters: a fictional Huang Shiren (a villain from the numerous revolutionary operas and the classic live-action movie *White-Haired Girl/Bai mao nü*, 1951, dir. Wang Bin, Shui Hua) and real-life historical figures: Liu Wencai ('commemorated' in the famous installation *Rent Collection Courtyard*)[12], and Zhou Bapi. Gao writes:

> The names of these landlords, as archetypes, pervaded the political vocabulary and historical imagination of the Mao era, so much so that Chinese who grew up after 1949 easily refer to these names when they think of the terms 'landlord' and 'old society',
>
> (131–132)

and adds later:

> The process of creating, revising, and contesting images of landlords with bad reputations in contemporary Chinese revolutionary art and literature reminds us of the Chinese revolution's character as an aesthetic movement, of a state-controlled network of cultural production, distribution, education, museumification, and of its foreign propaganda.
>
> (158)

Mao has 'refreshed' this symbolic reservoir when advancing a counter-attack on the political opponents who negated the sense of the Great Leap Forward and collectivization. In 1962, he advanced the call to 'never forget class struggle'.[13] You Lei's film may be read as a direct response to the Chairman's summon.

2.1.5 REVOLUTIONARY PEDAGOGICS

A corpus of texts related to the variations, adaptations, and editorial reviews of Gao Yubao's memoirs pronounced ideological meanings which belong to the discourses of education and upbringing campaigns. These movements are less often discussed by the cultural historians; nevertheless, they appear of significant importance for the Chinese animated film scholars since the major function of animation in the New China was to educate and socialize the youth. What is more, the fluctuations and dynamics of the propagated educational models allow one to approach one of the most critical phenomena of the Cultural Revolution, i.e., the Red Guards movement. The generation born during the Liberation period granted Mao Zedong a mass, fanatic support in the struggle with his political opponents. The revolutionary youth of the 1960s gained power over the society with the use of brutal means which have crystalized on the grounds of new social pedagogics.

The language reform and simplification of the Chinese characters which underwent in the first half of the 1950s have significantly helped in a struggle with illiteracy. As Kleemeier notes, Gao Yubao's memoirs played a pivotal part in propaganda discourse about the students' conscientiousness. Gao's obstinance in learning the characters was motivational and presented as a model behavior. Early publications of Gao Yubao's fiction functioned as an element in a wider, early 1950s' 'I Write about Myself' movement (*wo xie wo*) which was especially promoted among the young soldiers of the People's Liberation Army. Besides educational and indoctrinating aims, the campaign also encouraged denunciating those who have caused harm to the people in the past, thus a mass education in reading and writing became tightly connected with the anti-feudal movement. Bitter and often tragic stories of the past echoed loudly among constantly growing numbers of readers, consolidating collective identity on the basis of demanding retribution as an indispensable condition of the historical justice. In turn, such kind of an ideological stimulation has launched a potentially counter-revolutionary area. The society has focused its attention on the subject of individual suffering. So far anonymous figures of the oppressed and resistant soldiers, peasants, and workers were granted individual names, personal characters, and particular background stories. The power apparatus used the methods of criticism and self-criticism, developed in Yan'an, as controlling mechanisms; however, the successful struggle with illiteracy has empowered new subjective instances to exercise various forms of speech, and encouraged them to reach out for new conclusions.

A redefinition of the aims of the communication based on memoires and confessions was necessary in order to maintain purity of the ideological meanings. Such were the premises of the Socialist Education Movement (*shehuizhuyi jiaoyu yundong*), the campaign initiated in 1963, at the time when the struggle between the factions within the Party escalated. The leading political officials of the campaign were Liu Shaoqi and his wife, Wang Guangmei. Mao sought to overtake this movement and eventually reformulated its assumptions in 1965. Educational rectification was ideologically imprinted in the campaign, and with the focus switch, it was the group of revisionists who became its target. Widely defined, this group was composed not only of the critics of Mao's cultural, social, economic, and international politics but also of the people who did not reject the function of a traditional culture in establishing the new socialist society, those inclined to individualism, and those whose positions in a current social organization could have been traced back to the passed feudal and bourgeois order (office clerks, intellectual elites). At that historical moment (a prelude to the Cultural Revolution), the famous work method of understanding the workers and peasantry with the means of working together and sharing the living conditions has altered into a form of oppressive reeducation.

With the rise of the redefined social pedagogics, Gao Yubao's star started fading away. As a protagonist of the anti-feudal coming-of-age tale, he has slowly evaporated from the text. The narrative development still revolved around the conflict between the landlord Zhou Bapi and a boy named Gao, but the back story of this young and courageous teenager has become detached from the personal experience of the famous soldier. It seems highly significant that the film from 1964 never touches upon the subject of Gao's empowerment through education. In consequence, You Lei's film renounces the essence of the 1950s' Gao Yubao's writings as well as its ideological meaning within the then prevailing cultural model. The ideological premises of the film appear to reconcile with Jiang Qing's arguments ("the past serves the present" not as a source of knowledge or life-experience guidelines but as an allegory of the contemporary relevant issues).

Invalidating historical context of the animated adaptation's textual source for the sake of affirming purity of the revolutionary culture may be acknowledged as another device employed in the struggle with institutionalizing culture production that echoes bourgeois ideas. This device could have been utilized in anti-elitist revolt against cultural and social comprehension of such categories as tradition, authority, or hierarchy. In the film, Gao's path to education and self-development is limited to designing an act of vengeance and executing it with a physical force. Gao offers the group all his talents and intelligence and asks for nothing in return. His attitude and personality are presented to the young viewers as attractive and valuable, in this way 'new' Gao resembles more of the iconic comrade Lei Feng (the symbol of the campaign known as Learn from Lei Feng/*Xiang Lei Feng tongzhi xuexi*) than of a past pedagogical construct of Gao Yubao the soldier. Stefan Landsberger characterizes the ideological construction of

Lei Feng, and other role models promoted in the first half of the 1960s:

> The defining quality of these models was their embodiment of the 'spirit of a screw' (*luosiding jingshen*), a concept that was derived from Lei Feng's diary. Here, Lei compared a person's role in society to that of a screw in a machine, and he expressed his fervent desire to be such a 'never-rusting screw'. In behavioral terms, this was interpreted as blindly following the instructions from the Party and/or superiors and attachment to the larger group.[14]
>
> (LANDSBERGER, *THE DEIFICATION OF MAO* 146)

2.1.6 *ROOSTER CROWS AT MIDNIGHT* REVISITED

You Lei's film may be acknowledged as a phase in a specific ideological work which has become a finished project with the release of a still photography *lianhuanhua* of the 1973. The story illustrated with the film stills used expanded material from the SAFS. The animated film and *lianhuanhua* differ in regard to the construction of the sequences what affects narration. Above all, one discovers a significant shift in regard to the ideological theme of the story. If animated *Rooster* ... essentially speaks about anti-feudal struggle, the photographic story incorporates it as an element of a wider thematic *continuum* of a communist struggle for a national cause. The time framing is more concrete in *lianhuanhua* for the period 1931–1945 is mentioned here directly. The character of an Uncle Liu functions in the film as an informal leader of the field workers. His superior position is emphasized with a characteristic framing of Liu's puppet as powerful, strong, and monumental. Liu's serious, graceful, and contemplative face is presented in close-ups what accentuates the weight of his words. Uncle Liu in the *lianhuanhua* becomes an undercover agent of the CPC who attempts to revolt other farm workers. Several times the book displays a scene of the peasants sitting around Liu who explains Mao Zedong Thought to them. In the film's final scene, a beaten Zhou Bapi walks back home holding onto his wife's arm, and the field workers laugh vividly. The battle has been won, but what about the war? *Lianhuanhua* from 1973 offers a precise answer to this question. After the lynching, the workers gather under Liu's guidance and join the 8th Route Army ("The workers are in high spirits after giving Skinflint[15] his lesson. Liu Ta-hung points out, 'This is only the beginning. We have more and harder struggles to face. Let's go!'", *The Cock Crows at Midnight* 69).

Three photographs compose a meaningful coda. The first image presents a scene of the rich peasants' trial: the Zhou couple bent on their knees with heads down, while the soldiers and peasants gather around them. Standing in front of them, Gao stretches out his hand in an accusatory gesture. The gathering is presided by Liu from the heights of an improvised presidential stool. A description below the still reads: "The following year. Under the leadership of Chairman Mao and the Communist Party, the people's army defeats the Japanese invaders. Liu, Pao and the others indeed return, and the peasants try Skinflint for his crimes" (*The Cock Crows at Midnight* 72). From the perspective of the Maoist visual propaganda, this composition may serve as a perfect attempt in heroization of the Red Guard character. When critically decoded, this still – whose meaning is built upon fusion of a child's innocence, mob's anger, and brutal power of the rifles – appears plainly terrifying. Two latter images present the 8th Route Army soldiers marching through the mountains. The narrative drive of the images is based on traversing between full plane (showing the whole assembly) to the medium shot where Gao, wearing a uniform and holding a red flag, remains a central character.

On this final stage of the ideological utilizing of *Rooster Crows at Midnight* story, one observes the changes in the heroic paradigm which have occurred between the formative period of Liberation until the socially and culturally redefining moment of the Cultural Revolution. A new vision of the founding myth – i.e., the myth of 'struggle for Liberation' – assumes equation between nation-building struggle, Civil War, and contemporaneity. In such a light, the former enemies of China (among them traitors, owners and exploiters, imperialists, and colonizers) constantly generate a threat to the society; thus, the victory of 1949 has to be constantly updated and reconfirmed as a 'continuous revolution'. Such is the future of the Chinese nation – present children (the future leaders, cadres, and workers) are already the soldiers of an everlasting revolution. Individualism is excluded, even if it only aspires to enforce the righteous and correct ideological contents. The instances solely worth of an individual name are 'Communist Party of China' and 'Mao Zedong', while the individuals should aim to diffuse their identities in those two ideal entities. On the layer of visual representation, the myth detaches from its modernist roots. Figurative and stylistic tropes derived from modernist trends become eliminated since they suggest too multifaceted interpretative strategies. Conventions of realism that open up for reflexiveness and nostalgia should be remolded into a romantic, revolutionary experience and turned into model realism which equalizes image and idea. This imperative subjugates all applied means of expression: character design, camera movements, inside-frame compositions, the symbolism of the colors (predominance of a red hue), narrative motifs (rising sun), etc. You Lei's filmmaking skills convince the viewers to submit and find pleasure in the attractively filmed and animated fiction. The awareness regarding its propaganda aims, understanding of the ideological contents of the film, and acknowledging the historical and social contexts which have determined its message, turns viewership into a highly disturbing experience.

NOTES

1. In the first half of the 1960s, the helm of economic governance was overtaken by Liu Shaoqi, Zhou Enlai, and Deng Xiaoping. The policies they had designed, aimed at pulling China out of the

catastrophic condition caused by the state of famine by the end of the Great Leap Forward. Concurrently (until 1964), Mao Zedong has strengthened influences and relations with the military officials (especially with the marshal Lin Biao), intensely fostered cult of personality, and ideologically clarified anti-revisionist rhetoric as well as tactics of the planned campaign that would target the opposition tendencies in the Party.

2. Bogdan Góralczyk writes: "It was 1962 when Deng Xiaoping applied a conventional wisdom from his hometown Sichuan province to formulate the famous catchphrase: 'It doesn't matter whether a cat is black or white, as long as it catches mice'. (...) And in 1965 the Prime Minister Zhou Enlai posed a concept of 'four modernizations' of the state (agriculture, industry, national defense, science and education), however he did not manage to implement this idea into real political program" (30).
3. About Xia Yan see chapter *1.1.1 Unlikely Pioneers.*
4. Wang Zheng, the researcher of the Chinese cinema who applies feminist study perspectives, notices a characteristic contexture of the political and the personal: "An analysis of the sources of their antagonism illuminates the entwined and always messy arena of culture production, politics, and personal relations, and ultimately, the contentions underlying the metamorphosis of mainstream discourse in the mid-1960s" (199). Noticeably, films resonating with the critical realism tendency, aiming at reinterpretation of traditional culture patterns, adaptations of Republican-era literature and theatre plays, or depictions of the living conditions and cultural traditions of ethnic minorities were frequently subjected to severe ideological criticism. Filmmaking unambiguous in its representation of the classes, vision of history, goals, and directions of social aspirations was supposed to resist such 'dangerous' or 'deceptive' direction.
5. The discussed article is: Xia, Yan, "Raise Our Country's Cinematics to a Newer Level". *Hongqi*, no. 284 (1 October), 1961, pp.8–15. In 1998, in mainland China, the collected writings of Xia Yan were released in 2015, this publication was revised and the bibliography was added: Chen, Jian, and Oijia Chen, *Xia Yan zhuan* [*A Biography of Xia Yan*], Beijing Shyiue wenyi chubanshe, 2015. In the publications cited here, Paul Pickowicz and Wang Zheng discuss Xia Yan's influence on the shape of 1960s film production, and they both notice lack of film historians' in-depth reflection over this unique figure.

6. In 1963, Xia Yan initiated publication of the film history study *A History of the Development of Film in China* discussing the achievements of the pre-war cinema (*Zhongguo Dianying Fazhanshi*, edited by Cheng Jihua, China Film Press, 1963). In the same year, the students of the Beijing Film Academy attended the screenings in the frames of the wide retrospective *Excellent films of the 1930s* (see Wang 2009).
7. Chen Huangmei was a Yan'an veteran and a close collaborator of Xia Yan. Together with his prominent principal, Chen faced a long-term trial; their names were used in the caption of the purge undergoing among the film community.
8. Among the valuable English-language literature see: *Popular Chinese Literature and Performing Arts*, 1984; Yan and Gao, 1996; *China's Great Proletarian Cultural Revolution*, 2002; Roberts, 2010; Wang, 2014; Wang, 2017; Jiang Qing's biographies: Witke, 1977; Terrill, 1999.
9. Jiang Qing pointed out that 600 million of the workers, peasants, and soldiers were forced to find entertainment and education in the spectacles performed by 3,000 theatre groups active in the PRC. She outlined a very concrete goal for the artists: "May I ask which class stand you artists do take? And where is the artists' 'conscience' you always talk about? (…) We stress operas on revolutionary contemporary themes which reflect real life in the fifteen years since the founding of the Chinese People's Republic and which create images of contemporary revolutionary heroes of our operatic stage. (…) Moreover, we need to foster some pace-setters, to produce some historical operas which are really written from the standpoint of historical materialism and which can make the past serve the present" (2-3).
10. Jin Xi, Wan Chaochen, and Wang Shuchen also worked at this production.
11. "Before China's liberation in 1949 when the peasantry was ground down by the landlord class, there were countless incidents in which the peasants rose in heroic resistance. The story told here is about one such incident" (*The Cock Crows at Midnight* 5). This is how the still photography *lianhuanhua* opens, further, the story consistently leaves out any references to the real-life soldier Gao Yubao.
12. An installation of 114 clay sculptures mediates the story of atrocious acts and sexual perversions of Liu Wencai. This narrative exhibition was opened for the visitors in the former landlord's household in 1965 in Sichuan province.

13. This call preserved the dominance of the anti-revisionist and anti-capitalist rhetoric in the political discourse of the 1960s. This slogan not only connoted already established areas of reference but it also underlined the necessity to remain politically and socially alert and to accept new methods of class struggle that could uphold proletariat dictatorship as defined by Mao Zedong (see Young, 1986).
14. Other studies of Lei Feng's figure are: Barmé, 2000; Larson, 2008; Steen, 2014.
15. In the *lianhuanhua*, Zhou Bapi's character is named Skinflint.

REFERENCES

Barmé, Geremie R. *In the Red: On Contemporary Chinese Culture.* Columbia University Press, 2000.

China's Great Proletarian Cultural Revolution: Master Narratives and Post-Mao Counternarratives (Asia/Pacific/Perspectives), edited by Woei Lien Chong, Rowman & Littlefield Publishers, 2002.

Góralczyk, Bogdan. *Wielki renesans. Chińska transformacja i jej konsekwencje [Great Renaissance. Chinese Transformation and Its Impact].* Wydawnictwo Akademickie DIALOG, 2019.

Jiang, Qing [Chiang Ching]. *On the Revolution of Peking Opera – Speech Made in July 1964 at the Forum of Theatrical Workers Participating in the Festival of Peking Opera on Contemporary Themes.* Foreign Language Press, 1968.

Key Papers on Chinese Economic History Up to 1949. Vol. 1, edited by Michael Dillon, Global Oriental, 2008.

Kleemeier, Christine Jeanette. *A Study on the Modern Chinese Novel, "Gao Yubao" (《高玉宝》), and Its Author Gao Yubao (高玉宝).* 1981. The Faculty of Graduate Studies, Department of Asian Studies, The University of British Columbia, MA dissertation.

Landsberger, Stefan R. "The Deification of Mao: Religious Imagery and Practices during the Cultural Revolution and Beyond." *China's Great Proletarian Cultural Revolution: Master Narratives and Post-Mao Counternarratives (Asia/Pacific/Perspectives)*, edited by Woei Lien Chong, Rowman & Littlefield Publishers, 2002, pp. 139–184.

Landsberger, Stefan R. "The Chinese Art of Propaganda." *Catalogue of Mao and the Arts of New China Exhibition and Sale of Literature, Ceramics, Stone & Wood Carvings, Posters & Prints, including the Collection of Peter and Susan Wain*, Bloomsbury Auctions, 2009.

Larson, Wendy. *From Ah Q to Lei Feng: Freud and Revolutionary Spirit in 20th Century China*. Stanford University Press, 2008.

Pickowicz, Paul G. *China on Film: A Century of Exploration, Confrontation, and Controversy*. Rowman & Littlefield, 2013.

Popular Chinese Literature and Performing Arts in the People's Republic of China, 1949–1979, edited by Bonnie S. McDougall, University of California Press, 1984.

Roberts, Rosemary A. *Maoist Model Theatre: The Semiotics of Gender and Sexuality in the Chinese Cultural Revolution (1966–1976)*. BRILL, 2010.

Steen, Andreas. "'To Live is to Serve the People': The Spirit of Model Soldier Lei Feng in Postmodernity." *The Changing Landscape of China's Consumerism*, edited by Alison Hulme, Amsterdam, Boston, Cambridge et al., Chandos Publishing, 2014, pp. 151–175.

Terrill, Ross. *Madame Mao: The White Boned Demon*. Stanford University Press, 1999.

The Cock Crows at Midnight. Foreign Language Press, 1973.

Wang, Tuo. *The Cultural Revolution and Overacting: Dynamics between Politics and Performance*, edited by Lanham et al., Lexington Books, 2014.

Wang, Zheng. *Finding Women in the State. A Socialist Feminist Revolution in the People's Republic of China 1949–1964*. University of California Press, 2017.

Witke, Roxane. *Comrade Chiang Ch'ing*. Weidenfeld and Nicolson, 1977.

Wu, Gao. "The Social Construction and Deconstruction of Evil Landlords in Contemporary Chinese Fiction, Art, and Collective Memory." *Journal Title Modern Chinese Literature and Culture*, vol. 25, no. 1, 2013, pp. 131–164.

Young, Graham. "Mao Zedong and the Class Struggle in the Socialist Society." *The Australian Journal of Chinese Affairs*, vol. 16, 1986, pp. 41–80.

CHAPTER 2.2

"Bombard the Headquarters"

The Little 8th Route Army

The extent of destruction brought onto Chinese social and cultural tissue in the course of 'Mao's last revolution' (Macfarquhar and Schoenhals) has generated a multitude of overwhelming and long-term traumatic consequences. Studies in history and politics of the Cultural Revolution diligently reconstruct this period accounting for various events that have changed the dynamics of the ideological clash between the political factions, referring, e.g., to the announcements declared on the mass rallies and official meetings, contents of the Party's circulars and memos, proclamations delivered in a form of *dazibao* (big-character posters). The ramified and complex calendars of the events[1] are supplemented with the lists of names, dates, and statistics that enclose millions of individual lives marked by the experiences of tortures, imprisonment, reeducation, long-lasting public humiliation, hunger, illnesses, incapacitation, and deaths inflicted on the people by

DOI: 10.1201/9781003241607-7

the courts' order or by the hands of the self-proclaimed militias, resulting from suicide or physical and psychological degradation.[2] The political implications of Mao Zedong's policies at that time aimed at elimination of the leaders and circles considered by the Chairman as rivalry and undermining fundaments of the Maoist doctrine. Mao Zedong did not accept Nikita Khrushchev's policies of dismantling the Stalinist dictatorship (according to Maoists, this line was continued by Leonid Brezhnev). He was afraid that similar tendencies would emerge in the People's Republic of China (PRC). Mao considered the line of admitting to the errors and distortions an existential threat for the Party, doctrine, and himself – in his view, he remained an inseparable element of the party-state absolute.

2.2.1 IDEOLOGY AND ARTS OF THE CULTURAL REVOLUTION

The struggle of the 'two lines' (this slogan was popularized by Mao Zedong's faction in 1962)[3] pointed the masses and Communist Party of China's (CPC's) members' attention to the principles of the theory of contradictions. According to this view, the ruling party began to reproduce the bourgeois world order where the masses and elites negotiate the outreach of their influences by accommodating traditional values and possessed resources, and by exercising their capability to create convincing narratives about the future world organization. In the negotiation process, it is the elitist group that occupies the privileged position, having at their disposal the financial and social capital, thus quickly appearing plausible in their formulations. The masses define their aims only during the process. The return of such social organization mechanism affects the masses and destroys the efforts and achievements of the Chinese revolution. Liu Shaoqi, and later on Lin Biao, were among the most prominent Party leaders accused either of following Khrushchev's revisionism or 'following the capitalist road' (*zouzipai*), being denounced as heirs to the identity of traitors of the nation and class[4] or 'poisonous herbs' (*ducao*). Regardless of the distinguished or average social position of the accused ones, the new struggle aspired to eradicate their presence and lifetime achievements from the social reality and collective memory. The radical adherents of Mao Zedong transposed the political fight against the individuals to the combat over the meanings of universals. The theory of the 'continuous revolution' entered reflection on society, organizing work, and cultural activity. On June 1, 1966, Chen Boda (Mao's acolyte who himself fell a victim to the Cultural Revolution in 1970) called for a struggle against 'four olds' (*si jiu*) in the editorial of *People's Daily*,[5] i.e., against culture, tradition, customs, and ideas. This concept recalled the spirit of the May Fourth Movement and its radical discord with the Neo-Confucian order, but also it assumed that the former system has penetrated the New China's culture. As such it posed a continuous threat to the mass liberation. New Democracy and construction of socialism were only supposed to be phases on the path to communist China (or rather, specifically Maoist China). As soon as Mao Zedong Thought was ready to transcend to a new level of the construction process, it was a social duty to bid former ideas farewell without any regrets or hesitations. Attachment to the cultural tokens created on any previous stage appeared as treason.

Youth, and especially the party members' children, were supposed to become the new revolutionaries. To a large extent, their socialization was conducted by the public educational and care institutions. Educated within the New China school system, they were 'natives' of the various indoctrinatory discourses, their world views and historical memory were shaped according to heroic, communist narratives about the national cause funded upon nationalistic, anti-traditional, anti-imperialist, and anti-feudal contents. The students from Beijing formed the first, still underground, Red Guard squads (*hongweibing*) already on May 29, 1966. Mao himself had been addressing the revolted youth in a spirit evoked in his famous big-character poster *Bombard the Headquarters*.[6] Within two years, the groups would gather at mass rallies and transform themselves into a militant arm of the class justice. These formations were frequently shaken by inner conflicts,[7] but on the general level, they enjoyed personal support from Mao Zedong, Chen Boda, Jiang Qing, and her closest collaborators (the so-called Gang of Four/*siren bang*).[8] These youth were the target group of Marshal Lin Biao's (Vice Premier, Vice Chairman, and the Minister of Defense appointed as Mao's successor after elimination of Liu Shaoqi) 1964-edited collection of quotations from Mao's writing and speeches, *Red Book*. In consequence, the debates based on critical argumentation were replaced with automatized repetitions of memorized slogans published there. The enthusiasm demonstrated by the students gathered in August 1966 at the Tiananmen Square spread throughout the whole country. The Red Guards were encouraged to freely travel around China in order to carry on the revolution, the mass meetings with the beloved leader were organized, and all means necessary in the struggle with the enemies were allowed. By 1968, the direct political aims of the radical Maoists were achieved and a top-down instigated process of dismantling the Red Guards begun. The rebellious youth were sent away for reeducation.[9] In the so-called 'May Seventh Cadre Schools', the oppressors and their victims met again, and together with the local peasantry, they were all forced to coexist in the remote and economically undeveloped parts of China.

In its intellectual and artistic dimension, the decade of the 1980s was dominated by the attempts to recount the *zhiqing* generation[10] experience, whereby the operating visual codes and figures of literary representation were directly rooted in the culture texts created during the 'last revolution'. In a generalized view, the period of the Cultural Revolution is characterized by the lack of artistic creativity; however, the revolutionaries of that time (similarly to the soldiers of the National Salvation Movement) were highly productive in creating posters, caricatures, *lianhuanhua* as well as various decorated appliances.[11] The contents of the rebellion were transmitted with the use of the patterns codified in accordance with the requirements of the new model art, grounded particularly in performative arts (opera, ballet, theater), popular music (revolutionary songs), literature, and poetry. In the years 1966–1969, the forms of creativity that require a collective effort (e.g., film production) were put on hold. From the early 1970s, the experienced film studio workers began returning to production houses, and the studios started working efficiently again. The production at the Shanghai Animation Film Studio resumed in 1972. Films made at that time maintained aesthetic and narrative requirements of the model revolutionary art. As soon as the institutionalized culture production of the Cultural Revolution period had been restored, an intense work of petrification of the revolutionary symbolism commenced.

The globalization processes which would reformulate the operating mechanisms of the Chinese art market at the verge of the 20th and 21st century located the narratives and imageries of the Cultural Revolution within the postmodern paradigm. Frequently evoking the aesthetics of kitsch and an impression of nostalgia, the stories of the Cultural Revolution reached towards fundamentally ahistorical tendency of the recycling and reuse of the symbols. Such approach eventually leads to the neutralization of the momentousness of the collective work of trauma and relativization of the meanings accumulated within this particular subject in the collective imagination. As a consequence, the politicized interpretations of the visual and audiovisual culture texts, grounded in the iconography and storytelling of the Cultural Revolution, become an individual, private matter, a performative function of the discourse found on the borderland between art criticism and formulation of the world view argumentation.[12]

2.2.2 SAFS DURING THE CULTURAL REVOLUTION PERIOD

In the spirit of cinema being the most important of the arts (a thought attributed to Vladimir Lenin), the Maoist power apparatus focused its attention on the cinematographic institutions even before the Cultural Revolution's political agenda was established in 1966. Firstly, the 'Xia-Chen revisionist line' was targeted, and Jiang Qing proclaimed the senses and patterns of the model literature and arts. The criticism of Wu Han's stage drama *Hai Rui Dismissed from Office* in November 1965 was an inaugurating campaign of the Cultural Revolution. The general atmosphere among the film community was already tensed – Xia Yan, the powerful and, to some extent, liberal vice-minister, lost his position and influences between 1964 and 1965. A crackdown on 'artistic realism' and proclaimed dominance of the model art (interlacing revolutionary realism with revolutionary romanticism) affected all the film studios in Shanghai. This call was formulated by Mao Zedong during the Great Leap Forward:

> [Mao] called for the replacement of Soviet Socialist Realism with a 'fusion of revolutionary realism and revolutionary romanticism' in the arts. Or, as Guo Moruo explained it, 'revolutionary realism takes realism as its keynote, and blends it with romanticism', whereas 'revolutionary romanticism takes romanticism as its keynote, but blends it with realism'.
>
> (LANDSBERGER 6)

The Shanghai Animation Film Studio (SAFS) was not an exception. In 1964, Te Wei, the studio's leader, was summoned to perform multiple acts of self-criticism; during the following year, he was held under isolation and subjected to psychological tortures. He was allowed to return to the SAFS in 1966 only to become a target of the struggle sessions held at the studio, and later on sent away to the 'May Seventh Cadre School' (see Lent and Xu 98–99, 172). The majority of the creative and administrative staff shared a similar fate. As John A. Lent and Xu Ying note (172), at that time, the whole output of the studio production was withdrawn from the distribution with the exception of two films: Tang Cheng and

Qian Yunda's *Little Sisters of the Grassland* (1964, *Caoyuan yingxiong xiao jiemei*) and You Lei's *The Rooster Crows at Midnight*.

The year 1972 saw the first 'new-revolutionary' animated film. The opening credits of *After School* (*Fangxue yihou*) do not mention any individual filmmaker involved in the production. This ten-minute drawn animation portrays an ordinary life in a modern, big, and revolutionary city. All the school children are pioneers – they wear red scarfs, study science, listen to the war-veterans' stories, and exercise sports in a form of a quasi-military trainings. When the creepy character of an ugly old man disturbs little girls in the nearby residential area, the school kids deal fiercely with the intruder with no reservation for violence. The happy ending presents the children's column marching under the red flag towards the sun. Since 1973, the names of the directors and staff members returned to the credits. Among the filmmakers active at that time, we find a lot of cadres who worked at the SAFS in the so-called 'golden period' (1957–1964) but who did not occupy leading positions. In the 1980s, these animators have introduced new themes related to the current literary trends and modernized the established *minzu* style conventions. They have also represented Chinese animated cinema at the European festivals and initiated the processes of intercultural exchange. Among them, one should notice Hu Xionghua, the director of *Little Sentinel of East China Sea* (1973, *Donghai xiao shaobing*), a cut-out tale of the courageous siblings who defeated the spies from Taiwan. Hu together with Zhou Keqin created *Reed Hero* (1977, *Ludang xiao yingxiong*), another cut-out animation which invoked traditions of woodcut and told a story of a brave peasant boy fighting with the obese and cruel Japanese general. Hu Jinqing also used cut-out technique in *Bow and Arrow* (1974, *Dai xiang de gongjian*), a film picturing the adventures of heroic children fighting against the enemies of People's Liberation Army (PLA) in an impressive and spectacular winter landscape. Eventually, Te Wei's close artistic collaborators, Wang Shuchen and Yan Dingxian, directed a cell animation *Little Trumpeter* (1973, *Xiaohaoshou*) whose protagonist indulges in fantasizing about the soldiers setting the artifacts of the feudal culture ablaze and horse-chasing class enemies. Contrary to the above-mentioned films of Hu Xionghua, Hu Jinqing, Zhou Keqin, and Yan Dingxian that cannot be considered representative for any of these animators' *oeuvre*, You Lei's creative output of the period consists of the director's most significant achievements.

2.2.3 *THE LITTLE 8TH ROUTE ARMY*: A TWOFOLD PLOTLINE

In 1973, You Lei directed *The Little 8th Route Army*, the most emblematic animation of the Cultural Revolution period. Historical localization of the film's plot is not as vague as in the previously discussed films made in the former, socialist period. The enemies and the heroes are immediately defined by the voice-over narrator:

> It's been six years since the anti-Japan war started. The Japanese have been attacking our base this autumn. Today we're going to cut down their supply lines. In cooperation with the main force, we will defeat them. The army and the villagers have to be united and join this war.

The viewers enter the reality of the film in a *in medias res* mode. Panoramic traveling reveals a vast sorghum field where the characters of the peasants, soldiers, and children labor vigorously in the night. A boy Hu Zi, the protagonist of the film, sits atop the telephone pole waiting for the signal to cut the wires. Suddenly the shooting starts. The peasants and the soldiers successfully leave the area with loads of sacks of grain – this act of provisioning instigates the conflict which further drives the plotline. The Japanese, stationed at the nearby town, attempt to extort information about the grain whereabouts from the villagers. Firstly, they sent over the Chinese collaborators to spy on the farmers. However, the peasants closely cooperate with the PLA, and their leader, captain Yang, is a guest of honor of the village leader's household. The local children adore the captain, especially Hu Zi dreams about joining the ranks of the revolutionary army. Being too young and inexperienced, he has to settle for commandeering 'the little 8th Route Army', i.e., a group of his childhood friends. During one Japanese attack, Hu Zi's little sister is severely wounded. At this moment, the storytelling adopts a twofold trajectory.

On the one hand, the film maintains a convention of the adventurous war genre with a narrative drive focused on intrigues that secure grain in the possession of the Chinese people. The plot development relies on juxtaposing the events occurring at the village and the Japanese-occupied town, it involves multitude of characters, and its rhythm is dictated by the twists consistent with the cause-and-effect logic of the storytelling. Hu Zi functions in the plot as an agent of pivotal changes who successfully deceives spies and military personnel (among them a dangerous general). On this layer, *The Little 8th Route Army* appears as an adventurous narrative of an engaging plot; it aims at attracting young audiences by presenting a daring lead character. On the other hand, in parallel with entertaining features, the convention of the didactic film is being implemented. Along the plot progression, Hu Zi matures, his initial desire to avenge the family's suffering transforms into a dedication to fight for justice for all Chinese people. Captain Yang seemingly guides him through this process, but in fact it is Mao Zedong Thought that enlightens Hu Zi, and the character of Yang functions merely as its transmission belt. Yang thoroughly studies the Chairman's words, explains their meanings to the boy, the two discuss the problems of ideology and guerilla tactics. In such a light, *The Little 8th Route Army* appears as a 'Maoist textbook for the beginners'.

2.2.4 THE CONCEPT OF MODEL ART

You Lei's film is infused with the aesthetics and rhetoric of the model art defined by Jiang Qing. The quality of such artistic expression was supposed to emerge at the interface of revolutionary realism and revolutionary romanticism. In the eyes of the Maoists, critical social realism as well as socialist realism, being the precursor trends to the model revolutionary art, have not generated satisfying ideological effects. The tendency of critical realism implied agency of the characters with a nuanced set of attitudes and motivations thus offering an interpretive possibility for a 'bourgeois deviation'. Rigid binarism of the socialist realism curbed an emotive melodramatic quality which – in varied forms and with different intensity – remains an integral element of the Chinese narrative mechanisms.[13] The strategies of realist representation of the Maoist period overcame such shortcomings. Tang Xiaobing notices:

> socialist visual culture was of paradigmatic significance because it was centered on producing a new way of seeing. In this new visual order and practice, it was important not only to see with a socialist eye, but also to recognize and affirm socialism in everyday life. At issue were both how and what to see, which made the creation of a socialist visual culture a dynamic and continually interactive as well as reflective process.
>
> (22–23)

According to the guidelines established in Yan'an, and production methods formulated by Chen Bo'er, Yuan Muzhi, and their collaborators, the realist cinema of New China reached out for the 'real life stories'. In 1953, a catalog of recommended subjects was created; it also indicated production quota for particular themes (see Wang 184). The production process was of a collective character, the shooting was held in authentic locations, and the 'naturshchiks' (non-professional actors) frequently performed in the films. The revolutionary aspect of these realist productions was to be found in ideologized fictionalization and visual symbols derived from the communication conventions established in the times of the revolutionary struggle. Theoretically, the plot could have been built around the story highly distanced from a time/space of the war with Japan and Kuomintang, but its meanings had to be directly and accurately tied to the life experience and ideas of the class struggle. Animated film production of the 1950s and the early 1960s has applied such a revolutionary realism model in a large extent.

While analyzing Xie Jin's film *Two Stage Sisters*, Gina Marchetti characterizes narrative strategies of the revolutionary romanticism:

> The film's plot, for example, follows the trials of a young peasant woman, who, (...), almost magically transforms herself into a revolutionary heroine. With a few exceptions, *Two Stage Sisters* deals with crystal-clear conflicts, between masters and servants, lords and peasants, powerful men and helpless women, in which traditional power relations are overturned. As in all revolutionary romanticism, the revolution becomes the most important motive force for change. Its coming resolves virtually all of the narrative conflicts. (...) Individual concerns find public resolution in the political arena.[14]
>
> (69–70)

The film language submits to the quality of uniqueness imprinted in revolutionary romanticism. Jason McGrath analyzes specific devices, among them associative editing that supports melodramatic potency of the model. In the revolutionary realism paradigm, the ideas may be discussed by the characters or be present in the diegesis as symbols. Revolutionary romanticism favors extradiegetic sphere as a space of absolute values. A sudden appearance on the screen of the motifs infused with the ideological meanings but abstract to the plotline and diegetic reality (e.g., red flag, rising sun, suffering, noble faces, etc.) allows for a blissful encounter with a perfect reality of an absolute.

> The discourse must claim to represent an 'objective truth' outside of it [the film], but the very external nature of this

> truth renders it unrepresentable within the discourse – which is thus forced to resort to an array of rhetorical sleights of hand. (…) Furthermore, in revolutionary films and other narratives, fictional Communist protagonists often served as Mao surrogates, representing the party's access to the Truth through their own heroism and their possession of the socialist realist gaze.
>
> (MCGRATH 12)

Only at the plexus of these conventions of realism, the artists may arrive at the model performances – *yangbanxi*. Model revolutionary opera became a matrix for all narrative forms of the Cultural Revolution period. In July 1964, the opera festival of contemporary themes was held in Beijing. The presented thirty-five performances motivated Jiang Qing to express a conviction that widely understood narrative arts necessarily need to undergo a Maoist revolution. Originally, she found only eight opera works valuable.[15] Jiang personally attended to revising their scripts, choreography, and set design, and also regulated permission for a public presentation by reducing eligible titles to these chosen narratives. The selected and accepted performances became a source text for further visual and audiovisual adaptations. Until 1975, the preliminary selection was extended to the next seventeen titles (see Wang 2014). All the narratives reworked by Jiang Qing and her collaborators may be characterized by the textual presence of artistic strategies that not only define the characters' identity, but also clearly delineate the characters' relationship with the diegetic reality and extra-diegetic reality of the communist 'absolute'.

2.2.5 THE (IN)ANIMATED DEVICE OF IDEOLOGICAL EMPHASIS

Suppositionality of meanings, a strategy derived from traditional aesthetic reflection and opera convention, served the purpose of emphasizing such moments of the narrative flow when the ideal is revealed to the public eyes for a brief moment of time: "freezes revolutionary action, and universalizes the particular" (Teo, *Chinese Martial Arts Cinema* 43).[16] Jason McGrath argues that the *yangbanxi* model attests to the 'formalist drift' of Chinese revolutionary art. If examined from the perspective of the ideological criticism, such drift leads to self-annihilation of the art as the meanings become blurred and the form appears emotionally empty. He describes such films as "manifestations of the creeping vacuity and separation from lived experience of ideological rhetoric" (31–32).

Suppositionality convention relies on fixed mechanism that constructs movements determining all the interactions between the characters, their gestures and poses assumed (*liangxiang*).[17] Studying animation allows one to expand reflection on this specific kinetic strategy. An unexpected immobilization of the animated objects or camera movements may strengthen dynamic tensions within the (revolutionary) action. Animation aims at the deception of the viewer's senses by creating a perfect illusion of movement. Revolutionary animation attempts to create such a perfect illusion only in order to suspend it in front of the viewer's eyes, and by doing so, expressing an ideological emphasis. However, it has to be noted this manipulation does not possess a meta-filmic character, and so the film reality is not questioned by any means. In animation, the ability of film reality to appear completely motionless stands against the logic of the medium. In Chinese revolutionary animation, this filmic device enables the function of portraying a specific condition of a consciousness that may verify the interactions between the characters and their surroundings in terms of senseful/positive or meaningless/negative, and the criteria are derived from the ideological reflection.

The *Little 8th Route Army* is woven from the moments of action when the suppositionality effect comes into force. Let us look at the first scene when Hu Zi is waiting for a sign to cut down the telephone lines. Already at this moment the filmmakers expected the viewers to decode ideological senses of the presented reality. In a wide plane, a static camera shows a line of telephone poles rising up to the sky alike the ship masts. Hu Zi hangs onto the upper part of one of them. Earth remains unseen in the image, and an infinite sky is a surrounding reality of the character. After the cut, we look at the boy, the viewer's attention is captivated by his big, deep-set eyes, and wide, black eyebrows. He cranes his neck on full alert not to miss the awaited signal, his movements are quick and firm. In a few-seconds cutaway, we see the Japanese soldiers firing at the partisans and calling for the reinforcements. Fast cut to Hu Zi's face – but this time, we see it in a diagonal image shown from below in a big close-up. This is a moment of immobilization. It is extremely brief but clearly observable. When the boy cuts the wires, the camera rapidly zooms out in a movement as energetic and decisive as the gestures of the little soldier. Full attention, dedication, action, fighting the enemy – this what determines Hu Zi's way.

The freeze frame effect that serves an understanding of the narrative and propaganda intentions of the film can be found in numerous scenes conveying a direct agitation. For example, at some point Yang teaches Hu Zi about the necessity of curbing individualism. The boy thinks he is strong enough to join the army, and he strives to avenge his sister. Captain Yang asks him to prove his strength by throwing bigger and bigger rocks. Eventually, Hu Zi cannot move a large boulder block, and he is forced to ask for help from the soldiers training nearby. Hu Zi understands the sense of this trial when Yang says: "You can't win a revolution just by yourself. (…) So many people have been killed. This war is not just about you, there is a great animosity between the two classes, it is about our whole nation". A whip zoom arrives at Hu Zi's eyes as he comes to a halt. After a few telling seconds, the camera zooms out quickly. The motion/stillness relation – of puppets, camera, the viewer's gaze – evokes an impression of a breakthrough momentum. Only then Yang may continue his lecture: "We are going to defeat invaders, and build the new China. (...) Now, we both follow Chairman Mao's lead!" This scene is unequivocal in enunciating the most significant, even if simplified, interdependent dogma *continuum* of the Maoist revolution: nation building is a class struggle, the victory can be achieved only by uniting against the enemy, the unity of class and society demands rejection of individualism, all people unite in the name of the Party-Mao, and the Party-Mao works in the name of all people.

2.2.6 IDEOLOGICAL EMPHASIS DEPRIVED OF EMOTIONS

In the view of the above-discussed Maoist dogma *continuum*, it appears significant that Yang explains to Hu Zi the theory of a struggle with 'three big mountains': imperialism, feudalism, and bureaucratic capitalism. A metaphor of social concepts as mountains fought by an average man first appeared in July 1945, i.e., the period close to the film plot's timeline. In his closing remarks on the CPC's seventh national congress, Mao recalled a parable of the Foolish Old Man who wanted to overthrow the mountains:

> The Foolish Old Man replied, 'When I die, my sons will carry on; when they die, there will be my grandsons, and then their sons and grandsons, and so on to infinity. High as they are, the mountains cannot grow any higher and with every bit we dig, they will be that much lower. Why can't we clear them away?' Having refuted the Wise Old Man's wrong view, he went on digging every day, unshaken in his conviction. God was moved by this, (...). We must persevere and work unceasingly, and we, too, will touch God's heart. Our God is none other than the masses of the Chinese people.
>
> (MAO, *THE FOOLISH* 322)

The Fool was aided by the heaven because he was determined; thus, he showed more wisdom than a critical, rational sage. The 'evil mountains' of imperialism and feudalism discussed in 1945 were complemented with the 'third mountain' of bureaucratic capitalism in the period of the Anti-Rightists Campaign of 1957. In his writings of this period, Mao used the category of a 'poisonous weed' which has reemerged in the Cultural Revolution to denote an extreme and heinous transgression. The year 1957 was characterized by a strong anti-intellectual turn whose rhetoric was refreshed in the Cultural Revolution: "The intellectuals must transform themselves into proletarian intellectuals. There is no other way out for them" (Mao, *Beat Back the Attacks* 469).

In June 1957, the *People's Daily* published the famous article *On the Correct Handling of the Contradictions among the People*, the re-edited text was published again by this leading party-state medium in the first days of the Cultural Revolution. Its original thesis served as a theoretical framework for the new struggle (see Qiu 17–18). While Mao Zedong defined the Anti-Rightists Campaign as a political struggle, the 'last revolution' was supposed to be of a totalistic character. The return of capitalism, weakening of the proletariat dictatorship, and a confrontation of two lines within the party (communist and capitalist) – all these presumptions were operative in a decade earlier crackdown on the rightists, and in the mid-1960s they became revoked as a set of current concerns. On the one hand, this approach justified the necessity of implementing the 'continuous revolution' (political agenda), on the other, this discourse being reproduced in culture, education, and even private conversations, fostered a feeling of the history's 'grand finale'. Regardless of all empirically experienced variables, the revolution is in fact everlasting, and the same historical moment endures. As a consequence, the same aspirations and goals remain valid timelessly, the same group of enemies is targeted consistently, and the relation between an individual and a state is determined in a sanctioned and unchangeable manner. The reality of mankind may be set in tremor or stillness at will. It can be subjected to the most violent shocks only for the purpose of invalidation of any, even the tiniest, gestures or attitudes possibly able to procure a change. A once imposed dogma of an intact continuance of a specific order is conditioned by the demand for a constant update of the reality.

A film reality submitted to such a vision of history gravitates towards formalism. The conveyed ideology congeals in emphasis. Its meanings, reproduced in an infinite number of ritualized culture texts, become deprived of references in the realm of feelings, memories, desires, in other words, in the realm of principal impressions which unfold in the cinema. In a result of a formalist drift, the films do not make an emotional or intellectual impact on the viewers. The indoctrination may influence the individuals to such an extent that they will replace an empiric knowledge with an ideological phantasma (e.g., when equating concerns of the past with the current affairs, they doubtlessly accept all consequences resulting from this fact). Simultaneously, a quality of escapism related to the visual attractiveness (as in the case of *The Little 8th Route Army* which is an animated variant of the adventurous war movie) reduces the viewer's cognitive needs. An individual participates in cultural rituals subject to the dominant doctrine, e.g., by watching for years only the works of model art. Such culture texts affirm the state and its power apparatus; thus, an individual is capable of declaring their own affirmation for it in accordance with accepted narrative patterns or visualize their devotion with customary symbols. The viewers may appreciate the professionalization of production or use of innovative techniques and technologies, and find technical efficiency as a compensation for emotions. Perceiving the production and technological qualities as ultimate values eradicate the need for critical reading of the culture texts. An obtrusive presence of the ideology in the work becomes one of the components of a transparent realism convention. It appears that in 1973, You Lei consciously employed this strategy.

2.2.7 THE 'THREE PROMINENCES' PRINCIPLE IN YOU LEI'S VOCABULARY

You Lei as an animated film director proved to be an efficient craftsman. His skills are vividly demonstrated in the film's dynamic *mise-en-scène*. The puppets were designed in accordance with a 'three prominences' principle (*san tuchu*), i.e., a representation strategy accommodating the characters' appearances, lighting, image composition, etc. The positive characters had to appear as close (*jin*), big (*da*), and bright (*ming*), while the enemies were portrayed as distant (*yuan*), small (*xiao*), and dark (*hei*). On one of his missions, Hu Zi walks around the town, pretending to be a wandering cigarettes seller. A first shot in this scene presents his upper body in a big close-up, the camera slowly moves away, but Hu Zi, bathed in sun rays, remains a central figure of the image. White jacket, red shirt, head up – his figure dominates over the hunched passersby. When the camera moves away, the puppet of Hu Zi starts walking forward, thus keeping his central position in the foreground.

No viewer has any difficulty in recognizing the enemies' characters. The Chinese collaborator who sneaks into rebels' village appears for the first time on the screen as a tiny figurine, walking clumsily down the hill. The Kuomintang and Japanese soldiers are not much taller than the children's characters, all of them humped, inept, comically bulky. The collaborator wears a dark robe, his eyes are half-closed, and face is strangely distorted. Kuomintang militia in their black uniforms all look alike, their hands and legs shake heavily when they expect an encounter with the 8th Route Army. The Japanese general's clothing is not dark, but the ill intentions of this character are directly suggested by the Hitler-like toothbrush mustache, exaggerated, round belly, and a penchant for swinging the katana. Bleak spaces they inhabit are presented from unnatural angles making them grotesque or monstrous. Revolutionary 'typage' intensifies the ideological effects established on the grounds of an artistic communication within the propaganda aesthetics of the previous decades. In a pursuit for a comic relief, You Lei reenacted former, proven resolutions for the visual narrative. However, the 'three prominences' were not always applied in this film with a rigid consistency. Just as Zhou Bapi, the landlord from *Rooster Crows at Midnight*, the enemies frequently fall on their knees and become subjects of beating and mockery, at such moments their position in the frame composition is central for only from this perspective the viewer can fully see how low, weak, and pathetic they are.

Discussing the execution methods of the 'three prominences', Christopher J. Berry and Mary Ann Farquhar notice:

> This rule was achieved by marrying the operatic *liangxiang* with the cinematic gaze. A *liangxiang* is a frozen, sculptural pose that visually conveys 'archetypal images and emotions' on stage. In film, the full *liangxiang* close-up on the character's face (and especially the eyes) intensifies the emotional impact; we call this cinematic look the *liangxiang* gaze.
>
> (63)

The 'three prominences', being a quality of representation, was transposed to the cinema from the conventions of a traditional stage performance. For the successful implementation of the method, it was required to engage specifically cinematic means of expression. In a puppet film, the basic conveyor of this effect (the actor) is replaced with an object of a highly reduced body language and facial expression. In *The Little 8th Route Army*, these features are almost completely eliminated. The potency of *liangxiang* quality has been imprinted into character design of Hu Zi and Yang's faces, or to be precise: painted onto their eyes. With the use of typical operations – above all, the close-ups on the eyes – the filmmakers inform the viewers that a particular reaction of the character to the occurring situation should not be understood as a natural condition, but rather as a record of a new, conscious, enlightened view on the surrounding reality (*liangxiang* gaze).

At one moment Hu Zi finds himself at the Japanese general's office telling him a false story of a grain transportation. The boy gets carried away with his own words, he does not agree to belittle the power of the communist soldiers, and despite the tensions rising in the room, he keeps behaving in a blunt, arrogant manner. This is a moment when Hu Zi proves himself as a fighter for the cause. You Lei often employed fast camera movements. In this scene, the movements' vectors align with the direction of the boy's gaze when he observes his enemies. Close-ups on eyes emphasize emotions accompanying Hu Zi who confirms his loyalty to the communist ideas. The puppet's movement is seemingly simple (the boy only walks around the room) but at some point, it appears as a precisely orchestrated choreography. An image of the unique situation determined by the revolutionary idea emerges from the multilayered sum of commotions, pauses, and gazes. The character performs meaningful gestures in a slowdown mode, the camera movement 'freezes', a profound symbolism reveals from the close-ups on the character's eyes. All these operations open a potential space for *liangxiang.*

The fact of maintaining the 'three prominences' convention in the revolutionary film would not be that much interesting, if not for the director's observable inclination towards constructing quite impressive mass scenes. When Hu Zi's mother holds in her arms a wounded daughter, she is surrounded by a dozen or so peasant characters of various age and gender, first shown with a half close-up traveling shot, all of them big and bright in appearance. Similar examples can be found throughout the whole film. However, when the viewers watch mass scenes involving both positive and negative characters (fighting sequences), the situation gets complicated in an interesting way. Importantly, the final battle sequence is shot at the background of caves and canyons, the action is dynamized by the shootouts and explosions. It is necessary to acknowledge that the animating process of the mass scenes (involving the participation of more than five, moving puppets) remains a highly challenging production endeavor, and a great difficulty for the animators.[18] You Lei clung to the 'three prominences' principle in a scene initiating the final battle sequence: Japanese and Kuomintang soldiers fidget towards communists' base (not knowing they are approaching a trap); the communists (soldiers and peasants) hide in the bushes on the top of the hills. Shot in a bright light, the characters of the communist fighters quite literally overshadow the grotesque enemies who almost crawl through the dark glen. The communists begin the attack with the use of firearms and hand grenades. The panicked enemies attempt an escape, but all the retreating paths are cut off. The action runs fast at this point; the direction of the gaze of the firing characters (*liangxiang* effect) dynamically repositions the camera's points of view; it also dictates the rhythm of the editing. The Japanese soldiers' defeat is presented from behind their backs or with bird-eye shots, both devices suggestively belittle these characters. They fall in agony unable to stop the pressuring heroes. The camera observes closely how they convulse, the bits of puppets' bodies fly in the air, and from time to time the black smoke shrouds the image. But when the two squads confront each other on the ground, and the fight with the bayonets and machetes begin, the pragmatics of film language which 'reports' from the battlefield ousts the model convention of the 'three prominences'. In such scenes You Lei sought for shots that would capture the viewer's attention to the largest possible extent – he chose the ones featuring high levels of brutality.

2.2.8 RED GUARDS: THE RUTHLESS HEROES OF THE REVOLUTION

'Hu Zi's adventures in the land of revolution' are driven by diversified, aggressive visuality and varied motivations behind violent behaviors. Only in the first five minutes of the film, the young hero runs for life at the enemies' frontlines, and his little sister becomes heavily wounded. Hu Zi's greatest dream is to join the army; therefore, he enthusiastically embarks on following missions and actively participates in the fights on the battlefield. Such a level of brutalization of the children culture production of the Cultural Revolution period was not unprecedented (just to recall wartime stories about poor Shanghai orphan Sanmao). However, as Tang Xiaobing notes:

> The bombastic posters and graphics accentuating waves of mass mobilization signaled a further intensification of the revolutionary imperative of socialist visuality. Driven by war fantasies, modern day hero worship, and impatience with post-revolutionary everyday life, the explosive Cultural Revolution visual ephemera broadcast a violent grassroots rebellion that was clearly anti-institutional, anti-establishment, and yet endorsed by Mao Zedong, the supreme leader of the PRC and a visionary revolutionist.
>
> (11)

These remarks emphasize a fundamental contradiction which is inherent to the Cultural Revolution, but impossible to fully comprehend by the distant observers: the masses rebelled against both old and new culture as well as old and new state's institutions. For this purpose, they have entirely trusted one man who had built his worldview under the conditions of living in the former culture, who has been intellectually, politically, and organizationally establishing the new world order, and above all, whose whole persona embodied the new system. The masses not only submitted to him as faithful followers but also on his behalf spread chaos, fear, and violence. You Lei's film did not attempt to resolve this contradiction. The film rather attempted to assimilate the imagery of the masses into newly defined socio-cultural conditions, i.e., the moment when the Red Guards had just joined the group of the victims of the reeducation system.

At the times of You Lei's film production, the victims and perpetrators of the Cultural Revolution began returning to the quotidian life. 'Continuous revolution' dictatorship eased off its dictates over the sphere of private lives, regardless of being still prevailed over the public sphere. The animation studio in Shanghai, an entity that was centrally controlled and organized according to the paradigm of a communist studio production, has reassembled former working cadres of animators, directors, graphic artists, and technical staff. At the twilight of the 'decade of fear',[19] the new ideological goal of the animated production targeted an incorporation of the recent history's events into a well-established mythical narration about the 'pre-Liberation era'.

The strategies of representation and narration became subject to the newly delineated conventions of the model art, while the most controversial agents within new stories, the brutal children (Red Guards), became conscripted into the ranks of the myth's heroes. It is only natural for the children's animation studios to present the peers of their target audience as the films' protagonists. However, it appears significant that the daring, young heroes of SAFS' animations from 1972 to 1976 have been attributed with an inclination towards violence performed in the name of the nation and Mao Zedong. In *The Little 8th Route Army*, twice we watch the scenes where the group of kids armored with spars embellished with red ribbons, attack the Chinese traitor. In both scenes, the children surround the vicious character and aim the spars at him. At first it is only a game, a theater performed for the sake of conspiracy, and so eventually the children let the man go freely. At the second time, the captive is delivered to the soldiers. Hu Zi appears as a true Red Guard. Standing by the side of captain Yang, facing the Japanese general, he does not hesitate to fire his gun. In the battle finale, two shots are fired at the general. Yang's bullet hurts the official's hand, but it is Hu Zi who shoots at his heart. The Japanese general falls down in agony, his gestures and movements appear to be grotesque. At the same time Hu Zi and

Yang cheerfully embrace each other. This is the closure of Hu Zi's coming-of-age, revolutionary story. The film ends with a conventional scene of the PLA's soldiers marching forward. Before this typical image, we watch the village celebrating Hu Zi – the boy is being decorated with a red rosette and honorably enlisted to the revolutionary army. Such an ending seems to suggest that not only 'today's' Red Guards aspire to continue heroism of the soldiers from the mythologized wartime, but in fact they are equal to them.

The relationship between the vision of the history presented in You Lei's films and their historicized interpretation is narrowed down to the acts of direct agitation for particular, contemporary, political concepts. In *Rooster Crows at Midnight*, the theme of an emancipatory struggle against the feudal lords appears to be reformulated in terms of anti-individualistic theory, while in *The Little 8th Route Army*, the Mao Zedong Thought of the Cultural Revolution period is studied at the frontlines of the Sino-Japanese war. Rationale for such blend of artistic creativity and ideological work may be sought on the grounds of totalitarian character of the system within which the filmmakers have functioned. Nevertheless, You Lei's capability in adapting dominant patterns propagating extreme policies of Maoism is distinctively observable. In his films, even the most horrifying practices of the revolutionary era (among them, trials of the property owners during the land reform period, Red Guard movement) find their pleasing and entertaining imagery. Such, at least disturbing, filmmaking efficiency derives from You Lei's cinematic feeling for staging and competency in constructing a convincing, engaging storytelling with the use of the means of expression typical for the revolutionary cinema.

NOTES

1. See Yan and Gao, 1996; Guo et al. 2006; Teiewes and Sun, 2007; Dikötter, 2016. The official documents issued during the Cultural Revolution were reprinted in: Gray and Cavendish, 1968; *China's*

Cultural Revolution, 1996. Jin, 1999. Lowell, 2015 analyze agency of the Cultural Revolution's main actors (other than Mao Zedong). Detailed calendars of the events can be found in Daubier 1974.

2. Official statistic data of the victims of revolutionary struggles presented at the 'Gang of Four' trail counts 727,420 persecuted, 34,274 death casualties (Góralczyk 50). Many historians argue that these figures are understated; however, it is impossible to proceed with more precise estimations due to inaccessibility of the archives, questionability of the available materials, etc. It is important to remember that 'Cultural Revolution' functions as an umbrella term for various and numerous rectification campaigns imposed in a top-down manner but also instigated on the local level between quarreling factions within committees' units or particular Red Guard groups. Song Yongyi summarizes the state of research: "Owing to difficulties that scholars in and outside China encounter in accessing 'state secrets', the exact figure of the 'abnormal death' has become a recurring debate in the field of China studies. Estimates by various scholars range from one-half to eight million. According to Rummel's 1991 analysis, the figure should be around 7.73 million (Rummel, 1991: 253). In the following year, however, Harvard scholar John K. Fairbank arrived at a rough estimate of around one million (Fairbank, 1992: 402). Several years later, Ding Shu, an overseas Chinese scholar, disagreed with Rummel's conclusion by using diverse analyses, and estimated the figure to be around two to three million (Ding, 1999: 214). Recently, Andrew Walder and Su Yang contributed a much more detailed analysis of the death toll in China's rural areas based upon statistics drawn from 1,500 Chinese county annals. In their estimate, 'the number killed [was] between 750,000 and 1.5 million, with roughly equal numbers permanently injured' (Walder and Su, 2003). In a newly published biography of Mao Zedong by two UK authors, the estimated totality of death is discussed: 'at least 3 million people died violent deaths and post-Mao leaders acknowledged that 100 million people, one-ninth of the entire population, suffered in one way or another' (Chang and Halliday, 2005: 547). Interestingly, the reporter of a Hong Kong-based political journal released the classified official statistics, according to which nearly two million Chinese were killed and another 125 million were either persecuted or 'struggled against' (subjected to 'struggle sessions') as a result of the state-sponsored killings and atrocities committed during the Cultural Revolution (Cheng Min,

1996: 21–22). The average death toll based on the aforementioned six investigators' figures is nearly 2.95 million. Considering that the Cultural Revolution took place in China during a period when it was not invaded by other states, the number of victims estimated above is extremely high" (Song, "Chronology of Mass Killings during the Chinese Cultural Revolution (1966–1976)").

3. The meaning of the slogan was accentuated by Chen Boda in his speech *The Two Lines in the Great Proletarian Cultural Revolution* delivered on October 16, 1966. He targeted his criticism at Liu Shaoqi and Deng Xiaoping.
4. The so-called blood lineage theory (*xuetonglun*) gained popularity among the faction of the revolutionary offspring of the Party's prominent members. According to this concept, the context of the family's class status (including possibility of belonging of the previous generations of 'five black categories'/*heiwulei*) and the parents' participation (or lack of such) in the revolutionary struggle in the times prior to the Liberation determine individuals' identity and their actions (see Blood Lineage Theory 56–58; Jin 15–41).
5. In Beijing, this campaign began on August 19, 1966. The mentioned article was titled *Sweep Away All Cow Demons and Snake Spirits*.
6. "But in the last fifty days or so some leading comrades from the central down to the local levels have acted in a diametrically opposite way. Adopting the reactionary stand of the bourgeoisie, they have enforced a bourgeois dictatorship and struck down the surging movement of the great cultural revolution of the proletariat. (…) How poisonous!" (Mao, *Bombard The Headquarters*, 205–206).
7. Various factions belonging to the wide category of Red Guards gathered students and workers, they affirmed different visions of Maoism, and conjoined in vehement struggles with the means of propaganda materials but also physical violence and guerilla actions. The most famous struggle of the *hongweibing* groups was the so-called 'Hundred Day War' happening at the campus of Tsinghua University on April 23–July 26, 1968. William Hinton presented the testimonies of the participants (1972). The events, described in a convincing and poignant manner, serve as a departure point for a story development in the first volume of Liu Cixin's *Remembrance of Earth's Past* trilogy (*The Three-Body Problem*).
8. The group consisted of Jiang Qing, Zhang Chunqiao, Yao Wenyuan, Wang Hongwen. The trial proceedings of 1981 also accounted for

the actions of Chen Boda and Mao Yuanxin. The accused faced charges of conducting grave political mistakes as well developing and implementing criminal plans for political struggle.

9. Initiated in the second half of 1968, the campaign Up to the Mountains and Down to the Countryside (*shangshan xia xiang yundong*) lasted until 1980, it involved seventeen million of urban youth (see Guo et al. xxix).
10. The so-called 'sent-down generation'; in Chinese language it is referred to as *zhishi qingnian*, in its widest sense this term means 'educated youth'.
11. Stefan Landsberger points this out in numerous of his scholarly writings as well as popular articles. The study and curatorial research of Laura Pozzi from the Chinese University of Hong Kong appears significant. Pozzi verifies the factual data about the materials from the Cultural Revolution period deposited at her university. She recognizes new form of *manhua*. Pozzi writes: "They could be called 'cartoons' (*manhua*), a term that appropriately describes the satirical content of these pieces. However, the word *manhua* is very general, and it is used mostly to define images printed in newspapers" (188). This researcher analyzing "graphic art of the *hongweibing* groups" from Guangzhou proposes a new term: "caricature poster" (*fengci xuanchuanhua*).
12. Selected readings on the subject of postmodern paradigm in the Chinese culture production: Chow, 1995; Zhang, 1997; Barmé, 2000; *Cinema and Desire*, 2002.
13. See Browne, 1994; Silbergeld, 1999. Jason McGrath discussing the concern of melodramatic narrative forms in relation to the revolutionary culture noted: "As Mao put it in his talks at Yan'an, people need art in addition to their everyday lives precisely because 'although both are beautiful, life as reflected in works of literature and art can and ought to be on a higher plane, more intense, more concentrated, more typical, nearer the ideal, and therefore more universal than actual everyday life'" (7).
14. Marchetti argues that *Two Stage Sisters* merges the influences derived from the traditional opera art, social and aesthetic concepts postulated by the May Fourth Movement, and the Maoist paradigm of realism, she writes: "Like most Chinese films of its era, *Two Stage Sisters* walks a tightrope between indigenous dramatic forms and foreign influences, between revolutionary romanticism and what Godard has called 'Hollywood Mosfilm'" (70).

15. The operas: *Taking Tiger Mountain by Strategy* (*Zhiqu wei hushan*), *Raid on the White Tiger Regiment* (*Qixi baihu tuan*), *On the Docks* or *The Harbor* (*Hai gang*), *The Legend of the Red Lantern* (*Hong dengji*); the ballets: *White-Haired Girl*, *Red Detachment of Women* (*Hongse niangzi jun*); opera and symphony: *Shajiabang*.
16. Elsewhere, Teo elaborated on the relevance of this quality in opera films: "The art director Han Shangyi, also a veteran of the genre, and whose 1956 article on opera film style and form is now considered a standard text in Chinese film theory, described the opera film as 'an artistic unification between expressionism and realism' where expressionism (*xieyi*) is a property of the stage, and realism (*xieshi*) is a property of cinema, which basically defines the central problem of making an opera film. Han went on to elucidate the problem by touching on the more complex issues of *mise-en-scène* involving a union between 'scenic and performance space'" (Teo, The Opera Film in Chinese Cinema 211).
17. The concept of a *liangxiang* pose is well-grounded in the theory of the Chinese theater: "The *liangxiang* pose, which is held for several seconds, is the moment of expressing presence and the moment when the performer catches his breath (…) The term *liangxiang* means 'radiant, luminous appearance' – it is the moment when the performer must glow, send out the quality of presence termed *qi*. (…) the expression of *qi* (force) which captivates the spectator's gaze happens at the same point at which *qi* is returned or gathered" (Riley 212).
18. Barry Purves, the master of British puppet film, accounts for physical difficulties inherent to the animation of the scenes involving interactions of many puppets (see Purves 226).
19. In one of the first Polish scholarly articles on the subject of the Chinese cinema, Professor Alicja Helman used the phrase 'decade of fear' referring to the period of Cultural Revolution (see Helman, 2008).

REFERENCES

Barmé, Geremie R. *In the Red: On Contemporary Chinese Culture*. Columbia University Press, 2000.

Berry, Christopher J., Farquhar, Mary Ann. *China on Screen. Cinema and Nation*. Columbia University Press, 2006.

"Blood Lineage Theory". *Historical Dictionary of the Cultural Revolution*, edited by Guo Jian et al., Lanham et al., The Scarecrow Press Inc., 2006, pp. 56–58.

Browne, Nick. "Society and Subjectivity. On the Political Economy of Chinese Melodrama." *New Chinese Cinemas. Forms, Identities, Politics*, edited by Nick Browne, Paul G. Pickowicz, Vivian Sobchak, Ester Yau, Cambridge University Press, 1994, pp. 40–56.

China's Cultural Revolution, 1966–1969: Not a Dinner Party, edited by Michael Schoenhals, M.E. Sharpe, 1996.

Chow, Rey. *Primitive Passions. Visuality, Sexuality, Ethnography, and Contemporary Chinese Cinema*. Columbia University Press, 1995.

Cinema and Desire. Feminist Marxism and Cultural Politics in the Work of Dai Jinhua, edited by Jing Wang, Tani E. Barlow, Verso, 2002.

Daubier, Jean. *A History of Chinese Cultural Revolution*, translated by Richard Seaver, Vintage Books (Random House), 1974.

Dikötter, Frank. *The Cultural Revolution: A People's History, 1962–1976*. Bloomsbury Publishing, 2016.

Góralczyk, Bogdan. *Wielki renesans. Chińska transformacja i jej konsekwencje [Great Renaissance. Chinese Transformation and Its Impact]*. Wydawnictwo Akademickie DIALOG, 2019.

Gray, Jack, Cavendish, Patrick. *Chinese Communism in Crisis. Maoism and the Cultural Revolution*. Frederick A. Praeger Publishers, 1968.

Guo, Jian, Song, Yongyi, and Zhou, Yuan. *Historical Dictionary of the Cultural Revolution*, edited by Lanham, et al., The Scarecrow Press Inc., 2006.

Helman, Alicja. "Dekada strachu [Decade of Fear]." *Kwartalnik filmowy [Film Quarterly]*, no. 61, 2008, pp. 123–136.

Hinton, William. *Hundred Day War: Cultural Revolution at Tsinghua University*. Monthly Review Press, 1972.

Jin, Qiu. *The Culture of Power: The Lin Biao Incident in the Cultural Revolution*. Stanford University Press, 1999.

Key Papers on Chinese Economic History Up to 1949. Vol. 1, edited by Michael Dillon, Global Oriental, 2008, pp. 15–41.

Landsberger, Stefan R. "The Deification of Mao: Religious Imagery and Practices during the Cultural Revolution and Beyond." *China's Great Proletarian Cultural Revolution: Master Narratives and Post-Mao Counternarratives (Asia/Pacific/Perspectives)*, edited by Woei Lien Chong, Rowman & Littlefield Publishers, 2002, pp. 139–184.

Lent, John A., Xu, Ying. *Comics Art in China*. University Press of Mississippi, 2017.

Lowell, Dittmer. *Liu Shaoqi and the Chinese Cultural Revolution*. Routledge, 2015.

Macfarquhar, Roderick, Schoenhals, Michael. *Mao's Last Revolution*. The Belknap Press of Harvard University Press, 2006.

Mao, Zedong. "The Foolish Old Man Who Removed the Mountains (July 1945)." *Selected Works of Mao Tse-tung, vol. III*, Foreign Languages Press, 1965, pp. 321–324.

Mao, Zedong. "On the Correct Handling of the Contradictions among the People (February 1957; published June 1957)." *Selected Works of Mao Tse-tung, vol. V*, Foreign Languages Press, 1978, pp. 384–421.

Mao, Zedong. "Beat Back the Attacks of the Bourgeois Rightists (July 1957)." *Selected Works of Mao Tse-tung, vol. V*, Foreign Languages Press, 1978, pp. 457–472.

Mao, Zedong. "Bombard The Headquarters – My First Big-Character Poster (August 1966)." *Selected Works of Mao Tse-tung, vol. IX*, Sramikavarga Prachuranalu, 1999, pp. 205–206.

Marchetti, Gina. "Two Stage Sisters: The Blossoming of a Revolutionary Aesthetic." *Transnational Chinese Cinemas. Identity, Nationhood, Gender*, edited by Sheldon Hsiao-peng Lu, University of Hawaii Press, 1997, pp. 59–80.

McGrath, Jason. "Cultural Revolution Model Opera Films and the Realist Tradition in Chinese Cinema." *The Opera Quarterly*, vol. 26, no. 2–3, 2010, pp. 343–376.

Pozzi, Laura. "The Cultural Revolution in Images: Caricature Posters from Guangzhou, 1966–1977." *Cross-Currents. East Asian History and Culture Review*, no. 27, 2018, pp. 187–207.

Purves, Barry J. C., *Stop Motion. Passion, Process and Performance*. Focal Press (Elsevier), 2008.

Riley, Jo. *Chinese Theater and the Actor in Performance*. Cambridge University Press, 1997.

Silbergeld, Jerome. *China into Film. Frames of Reference in Contemporary Chinese Cinema*. Reaktion Books, 1999.

Song, Yongyi. *Chronology of Mass Killings during the Chinese Cultural Revolution (1966–1976)*. Online Encyclopedia of Mass Violence, 2011, www.sciencespo.fr/mass-violence-war-massacre-resistance/en/document/chronology-mass-killings-during-chinese-cultural-revolution-1966-1976. Accessed 3 Jan. 2021.

Tang, Xiaobing. *Visual Culture in Contemporary China. Paradigms and Shifts*. Cambridge University Press, 2015.

Teiewes, Frederick C., and Sun, Warren. *The End of the Maoist Era. Chinese Politics during the Twilight of the Cultural Revolution, 1972–1976*. M. E. Sharpe, 2007.

Teo, Stephen. *Chinese Martial Arts Cinema. The* Wuxia *Tradition.* Edinburgh University Press, 2009.

Teo, Stephen. "The Opera Film in Chinese Cinema: Cultural Nationalism and Cinematic Form." *The Oxford Handbook of Chinese Cinemas*, edited by Carlos Rojas, Oxford University Press, 2013, pp. 209–224.

Wang, Zheng. *Finding Women in the State. A Socialist Feminist Revolution in the People's Republic of China 1949–1964.* University of California Press, 2017.

Yan, Jiaqi, and Gao, Gao. *Turbulent Decade: A History of the Cultural Revolution.* University of Hawaii Press, 1996.

Zhang, Xudong. *Chinese Modernism in the Era of Reforms. Cultural Fever, Avant-Garde Fiction, and the New Chinese Cinema.* Duke University Press, 1997.

Final Notes

The 'myth of origin' that is manifested in Maoist animated production is constructed in the following way: realistic depiction appears as a particular account of the history. The subject matter of the films refers to the characters and events archetypal for the established vision of the Chinese revolution history. Chiang Kai-shek, Sanmao, Zhou Bapi, Gao Yubao, soldiers of the 8th Route Army – all of them belong to the pantheon of heroes and villains of the collective historical memory. However, the practice of 'accounting for the facts' does not seem enough to consolidate the imposed vision of history. Revolutionary art ideologizes this vision in compliance with the ever-evolving doctrine, even at the cost of negating historical meanings of the delivered stories.

At the dawn of establishing the socialist cinema structures, the aesthetic and intellectual choices of the filmmakers frequently derived from their personal experiences of resistance. Such individualization bears a risk of an emergence of certain cognitive dissonances. In *The Emperor's Dream*, the filmmakers' intention was to portray a moral degeneration of Chiang Kai-shek, and for this purpose, they have positioned a caricatural villain on the opera stage. Performative traditions were denunciated as 'old' and 'corroded'; however, the same traditions provided the authors with the means of expression needed for creating unique and eerie poetics of the film. Just before the Great Leap Forward, *Wanderings of Sanmao* were meant to remind the people about the primacy of class solidarity and common struggle against the bourgeoise, capital owners, and traitors, and the figure of the famous orphan straying in Shanghai under Kuomintang's rule embodied this message. The represented reality was characterized as oppressive and brutal; however, this impression was contradicted with the appearance of a nostalgia inherent to the protagonist himself.

Revolutionary culture has radically changed conditions of conceptualizing and producing animated propaganda. In You Lei's films, the representation of factual events (e.g., anti-feudal resistance, guerilla war with the Japanese) fully complies with narrative, representational, and indoctrinating mechanisms developed at the times of the films' production. Historical disguise allows one to equate the prior to the 1949-Liberation contents of the doctrine with those accepted by the New China's people as fundamental and formative. Propaganda animation of the Cultural Revolution assumes as fact that Mao Zedong and the communist army achieved great revolution, and at the same time, it assumes that the great revolution once achieved, never becomes a stable and fixed fact. The desire of revolution's intact continuity requires its constant relaunch and reoccurrence. A mythologized storytelling needs to follow the pattern of revolution's unfolding, reproduce it, submit and verify it with ever-changing, new requisites encountered at the revolution's following stages.

The question about the relationship between the fictional reality of the animated film and the historical reality contains a discussion about the status of history formulated under the conditions of mass-culture production defined by a totalitarian regime as a device of children's indoctrination. Mimetic conventions filtered through recognizable codes of communication of traditional narrative as well as visual and performative expression are elemental artistic methods that construct this relationship. Qualities related tightly to the specificities of the film language began playing a significant role only in the late Maoist period. Chen Bo'er and Tadahito Mochinaga's *The Emperor's Dream* (1947) meets the children production generic and pedagogical criteria in the smallest degree. Its main target group was the soldiers and the inhabitants of the territories newly acquired by the communist army. At that time, the viewers only began the process of evaluating communist propaganda narrative and visual communication codes as dominant (i.e., comprehensively depicting and explaining the surrounding, empiric reality). In *Wanderings of Sanmao* (1958) Zhang Chaoqun and Zhang Leping have built a bridge between ideologized rhetoric of New China and the viewers' collective memory of past images and narrations. In doing so, they reached towards the heritage of *manhua* of the National Salvation Movement struggle when conventions of modernism became subjected to the nationalistic agenda of mass, militant mobilization. Formally attractive and professionally executed films of You Lei (*Rooster Crows at Midnight*, 1964; *The 8th Little Route Army*, 1973) adhere to the concept that the Maoist narrative "treats children as adults and adults as children" (Diény 8 qtd. in Wu 47),[1] in other words, these films assumed existence of only one possible, receiving instance which fully accepts the ritualization as a method of realism in (animated) cinema.

The diverse variations of the Maoist realism are subjugated to the sphere of ideological meanings, which determine the films' relations with historical reality. On the following phases of building socialism and mounting a communist revolution, the vision of history has undergone updates complying with the then-current requirements of political and ideological nature. Today's *raison d' état* may immediately become a rationale of a regressive and repulsive past. The operation of historicization of the films' contents consists of two complementary mechanisms: mythicization of the historical narratives and modification of the history. In so doing, the propaganda creators may supersede the viewers' interest in the mechanisms of remembering, revising, and verifying. The 'founding myth' (a relative safe-zone of artistic creativity) expresses the contents that enable the viewers to define and valuate the most significant events of the past, but above all, this myth explicates ideological meanings of the current events experienced empirically. Simultaneous mythicization and modification (update) of the vision of the past is a strategy that remerges anew on following phases of political and cultural history. On the layer of rhetoric and symbolism, the same mythologized formulations are reproduced in a ritualized manner. On a layer of ideologization (highly important as it contains the promise of encountering the 'absolute' of the doctrine), the current political aims are formulated as truths of a formative character, each time potent to redefine the communist society as a unique mass that has integrated class, nationhood, and world view.

The films which have guided us through the intricacies of historical and ideological development of Shanghai Animation Film Studio (SAFS) in the Maoist period thematize and represent historical events and characters. A diachronic perspective allows one to delineate the phases of negotiations occurring at the 'artistic frontline' between the postulates of depicting history in a realistic mode and the necessity to establish Chinese paradigm of realism. Animation was challenged to renounce socialist realism, overcome its own fantastical qualities, and conform to acceptable conventions of representation and discourse (bigger-than-life images that derive from the real life). *The Emperor's Dream* and *Wanderings of Sanmao* share the attempt to transgress a binarism immanent to propaganda ('us-them') through a full, narrative, and visual focus on only one out of two potential realities. In the examined extract from *The Emperor's Dream*, nothing else than the degenerated world of Chiang Kai-shek, his American allies, and Chinese traitors exist. Less extreme in this sense, *Wanderings of Sanmao* depicts an oppressive and miserable world but the meaningful interactions may occur only in a positively valuated reality where the poor and heroic characters unite. Visuals and storytelling in Chen Bo'er's 'extravaganza propaganda' present the historical events and characters as caricatures. Nostalgia apparent in Zhang Chaoqun's film counter-balances the intensely bitter social reality of the Chinese 'sciuscià'. In regard to both films, one may argue that up until the late 1950s, a directly agitating animated propaganda used the mechanism of modification of the history on the basis of visual and narrative strategies established at the historical moments the films represented.

The vision of the revolutionary war became reworked – reimagined anew – in the 1960s. The then artistic policy of the Shanghai studio balanced between a requirement of engaging in political struggle and a need of exploring aesthetic qualities of animated film medium. It seems that You Lei's films contributed to the professionalization of the production mechanisms. At this stage, Chinese animated films thematizing history would assimilate rhetoric and symbolics through which dramatic events and tragic characters (e.g., trials of the land owners, struggle sessions, Red Guards' activities) would acquire attributes and identifications enabling their immediate and fixed, heroic recognition in a continuum of a mythicized nation cause struggle. What is more, in *Rooster Crows at Midnight* narrative motifs of individualization, emancipation, and empowerment, significant for the source text, became eradicated. It is, however, *The Little 8th Route Army* where the empiric reasoning was replaced with ideological abstracts in the most complete way. Employed model convention of *yangbanxi* appeared powerful as You Lei adapted several live-action cinema's strategies of expression and rejected 'old' communication methods derived from visual arts. However, the extreme formalist drift inevitably 'froze' engaging capacities of the directly agitating, animated propaganda.

The revolutionary model of animation assumed the viewer's readiness to accept ideological contents as absolute truths. After Mao Zedong's death in 1976, the concept of artistic expression as an encounter with a communist 'absolute' became deprived of its integral element that merged Maoist propaganda art with an empiric world. The mausoleum replaced the vital power of the doctrine. Until that time, Mao's portraits and his various representations (slogans and citations included) consistently and efficiently compensated for individualized discourses. After the leader's death, the cinema production apparatus (subjugated to the doctrine which itself has been undergoing redefinition) began to 'de-freeze' its inherent, propaganda mechanisms in regard to the ideas of realism, authenticity, and historical credibility. Since the 1940s, the conventions of realism had been acknowledged as fundamental and only valuable paradigms of artistic creativity. The demands of the doctrine erased potencies of psychologization and criticism – the list of the encouraged, 'real life' subjects was complemented with a uniformity of storytelling solutions, while applied visuality received a limited pool of interpretations. At the same time, these ideologically motivated, reductionist procedures were aimed at continuous stimulation of the masses' belief in the doctrine. Their operative devices included direct agitation, pathos, emphasis, contemptuous mockery, and even brutality.

Animated film of the Maoist period, similarly to live-action cinema, appears paradoxical. Filmmaking creativity seems driven by the need to express highly engaging, dramatic, and revolutionary tensions that can only be solved by reproducing the doctrine's contents in its visual and textual body. These contents, however, invalidated qualities of the empiric world, and eventually they terminated their own referentiality as truthful depictions of reality, relations, and interactions occurring within reality. In the new era of 'reforms and opening-up', propaganda films had to adapt fast to the new definitions of authenticity. At this stage though both the filmmakers and the viewers have already acknowledged the existence of a thin, red line delineating the ritualized filmic reality from the dynamics of real emotions which cinema is potent to awake.

NOTE

1. Du (2019, 10) contends this widely assimilated view and presents nuancing statement recalling coverage of You Lei's *Rooster* … in *Film Art* (*Dianying yishu*) from March 1965. She acknowledges the fact that the children in the audience mocked the film and its characters. This is a valuable notion that contributes to the studies on reception of animated film.

REFERENCES

Diény, Jean-Pierre. *Le monde est à vous: la Chine et les livres pour enfants.* Gallimard, 1971.

Du, Daisy Yan. *Animated Encounters: Transnational Movements of Chinese Animation, 1940s-1970s.* University of Hawaii Press, 2019.

visualizingcultures.mit.edu/modern_sketch/ms_essay01.html. Accessed: 15 Dec. 2021.

Wu, Weihua, "In Memory of Meishu Film: Catachresis and Metaphor in Theorizing Chinese Animation." *Animation Interdisciplinary Journal* (Sage), vol. 4, no. 1, 2009, pp. 32–52.

Glossary

A Da (Xu Jingda)	阿 达 （徐 景 达）
Ai Qing	艾 青
An Xu	安 旭
Babai zhanshi	《八 百 壯 士》
Bai mao nü	《白 毛 女》
baihuaqifang, baijiazhengming	百 花 齐 放 、百 家 争鸣
bainian gouchi	百 年 国 耻
Balu jun	八 路 军
banhua	版 画
Banye ji jiao	《半 夜 鸡 叫》
Cao ren	《草 人》
Caoyuan yingxiong xiao jiemei	《草 原 英 雄 小 姐 妹》
changzheng	长 征
Chen Boda	陈 伯 达
Chen Bo'er	陈 波 儿
Chen Duxiu	陳 獨 秀,
Chen Huangmei	陈 荒 煤
Chen Juanyin	陳 涓 隱
Chen Xi	陈 曦
Chen Zhihong	陈 志 宏
Chiang Kai-shek (Jiang Jieshi, Jiang Zhongzheng)	蔣 介 石, 蔣 中正
chusi hai	除 四 害
da	大

Da Maque 《打麻雀》
Danao tiangong 《大闹天宫》
Da yu haitang 《大鱼海棠》
Da yuejin 大跃进
Dagongbao 《大公報》
Dai xiang de gongjian 《带响的弓箭》
Dalu de gushi 《大橹的故事》
dazibao 大字报
Deng Xiaoping 邓小平
Dongguo xiansheng 《东郭先生》
donghua zuo minzu hua daolu 动画走民族化道路
Duan Xiaoxuan 段孝萱
ducao 毒草
Duli manhua 《独立漫画》
Duoluo 《堕落》
Dushi fengguang 《都市風光》
Fang Ming 方明
Fangxue yihou 《放学以后》
fanyou yundong 反右运动
Feng Zikai 丰子恺
fengci xuanchuanhua 讽刺宣传画
Funü shenghuo 《妇女生活》
gaizao 改造
Gao Yubao 高玉宝
Geming jiating 《革命家庭》
Guo Moruo 郭沫若
guoqing 国情
Hai gang 《海港》
Hai Rui baguan 《海瑞罢官》
hanjian 汉奸
hei 黑
heiwulei 黑五类
Hengsao yiqie niuguisheshen 《横扫一切牛鬼蛇神》
Hepingge 《和平哥》

Hong dengji	《红灯记》
Hongjun qiao	《红军桥》
Hongqi	《红旗》)
Hongse niangzi jun	《红色娘子军》
hongweibing	红卫兵
Hongzha	《轰炸》
Houzi lao yue	《猴子捞月》
Huang Shiren	黄世仁
Hu Jinqing	胡进庆
Hu Xionghua	胡雄华
Hua Junwu	华君武
Huangdi meng	《皇帝梦》
Huo yan shan	《火焰山》
Huoshao honglian si	《火烧红莲寺》
Jiang Qing	江青
Jiefangjun wenyi	《解放军文艺》
jin	近
Jin Xi	靳夕
Jiuwang manhua	《救亡漫画》
Jiuwang manhua xuanchuandui	救亡漫画宣传队
jiuwang yundong	救亡运动
jixu geming lun	继续革命论
Kangzhan manhua	《抗战漫画》
katong	卡通
Kongque gongzhu	《孔雀公主》
Kuomintang	國民黨
Lei Feng	雷锋
Lei Lei	雷磊
Li Baochuan	李保传
Li Dazhao	李大釗
Li Keran	李可染
Li kezhang qiao nan chuishi ban	《李科长巧难炊事班》
Liang Xuan	梁旋
liangtiao luxiang douzheng	两条路线斗争

liangxiang	亮相
lianhuanhua	连环画
lilun	理论
Lin Biao	林彪
Lin Wenxiao	林文肖
Liu Shaoqi	刘少奇
Liu Wencai	刘文彩
Lu Xun	鲁迅
Ludang xiao yingxiong	《芦荡小英雄》
luosiding jingshen	螺丝钉精神
Ma Kexuan	马克宣
Makesi-liening zhuyi	马克思列宁主义
Mandiao	慢雕
manhua	漫画
Mao Yuanxin	毛远新
Mao Zedong sixiang	毛泽东思想
Mao Zedong	毛泽东
Mao Zhuxi yulu	《毛主席语录》
meishu pian	美术片
ming	明
minsheng	民生
minzhu	民主
Minzhu dongbei di si ji (10): Huangdi meng	《民主东北第四辑（10）：皇帝梦》
Minzu	民族
Mudi	《牧笛》
Mu'ou yingpian	木偶影片
Muyang shaonian	《牧羊少年》
Nezha nao hai	《哪吒闹海》
nianhua	年画
Qi Baishi	齐白石
Qian Jiajun	钱家骏
Qian Yunda	钱运达
Qingchun xian	《青春线》

Qixi baihu tuan	《奇袭白虎团》
Qu Qiubai	瞿秋白
san tuchu	三突出
san zuo dashan	三座大山
Sang Hu	桑弧
Sanmao congjunji	《三毛从军记》
Sanmao liulang ji	《三毛流浪記》
sanmin zhuyi	三民主义
Shajiabang	《沙家浜》
Shanghai Manhua	《上海漫画》
Shanghai meishu dianying zhipian chang	上海美术电影制片厂
Shanghai po ke	《上海潑克》
Shangshan xiaxiang yundong	上山下乡运动
Shanshui qing	《山水情》
shehuizhuyi jiaoyu yundong	社会主义教育运动
Shen Bochen	沈泊尘
Shenbi	《神笔》
Shengsi tongxin	《生死同心》
Shidai manhua	《时代漫画》
shiyan	实验
Shouzu yuan	《收租院》
Shuangjiang	《霜降》
Shui Hua	水华
Si jiu	四旧
Siren bang	四人帮
sixiang	思想
Su Da	速达
Sun Xun	孙逊
Sun Yat-sen (Sun Zhongshan)	孫中山
Sun Yu	孙瑜
Tang Cheng	唐澄
Tao Jin	陶金
Taoli jie	《桃李劫》
Te Wei	特伟

Tian Xiaopeng	田晓鹏
Tie shan gongzhu	《铁扇公主》
Wan Chaochen	万超尘
Wan Dihuan	万涤寰
Wan Guchan	万古蟾
Wan Laiming	万籁鸣
Wang Bin	王滨
Wang Guangmei	王光美
Wang Hongwen	王洪文
Wang Longji	王龍基
Wang Shuchen	王树忱
Wang xiansheng	《王先生》
Wengzhongzhuobie	《瓮中捉鳖》
Wenhua dageming	文化大革命
wo xie wo	我写我
Wu Han	吴晗
Wu qi gan xiao	五七干校
Wu Xun Zhuan	《武训传》
Wusi yundong	五四运动
Wutai jiemei	《舞台姐妹》
xia shenghuo	下生活
Xia Yan	夏衍
xiang Lei Feng tongzhi xuexi	向雷锋同志学习
xiao	小
Xiao balu	《小八路》
Xiao kedou zhao mama	《小蝌蚪找妈》
Xiaochenabo	《小晨報》
Xiaohaoshou	《小号手》
Xie Jin	谢晋
Xie Tieli	谢铁骊
xieshi	寫實
xieyi	寫意
Xin qingnian	《新青年》
Xin wenhua yundong	新文化運動
Xin Zhongguo	新中国

Xinhai geming	辛亥革命
xinmanhua	新漫画
Xiyou ji	《西游记》
Xiyou ji zhi dasheng guilai	《西游记之大圣归来》
Xiyou manji	《西遊漫記》
Xu Bingduo	许秉铎
Xue Yanping	薛燕平
xuetonglun	血统论
Yan Dingxian	严定宪
Yan Gong	嚴恭
Yan Shanchun	阎善春
Yan Zheguang	虞哲光
yangbanxi	样板戏
Yao Wenyuan	姚文元
Ye Qianyu	叶浅予
Ye you epiao	《野有饿殍》
Ying Yunwei	应云卫
You Lei	尤磊
yuan	远
Yuan Muzhi	袁牧之
Zaochun eryue	《早春二月》
Zhang Chaoqun	章超羣
Zhang Chun	张春
Zhang Chunqiao	张春桥
Zhang Ding	张仃
Zhang Guangyu	张光宇
Zhang Huilin	張慧臨
Zhang Leping	张乐平
Zhang Shichuan	张石川
Zhang Songlin	张松林
Zhang Zhengyu	张正宇
Zhao Ming	趙明
Zhengxue	政學派
Zhiqu wei hushan	《智取威虎山》
zhishi qingnian (zhiqing)	知識青年

Zhiyong Zhiren	持永只仁
Zhongguo Gongchandang	中国共产党
Zhongguo minzhu shehuidang	中国民主社会党
Zhongguo qingnian dang	中国青年党
Zhonghua minzu weida fuxing	中华民族伟大复兴
Zhonghua minguo	中華民國
Zhonghua Renmin Gongheguo	中华人民共和国
Zhongyang Wenge Xiaozu	中央文革小组
Zhou Bapi	周扒皮
Zhou Enlai	周恩来
Zhou Keqin	周克勤
Zhu fu	《祝福》
zouzipai	走资派

Index

D

E

N

O

P

Q

R

Printed in the United States
by Baker & Taylor Publisher Services